CONTENTS

Public Literacy

Second Edition

Elizabeth Ervin
University of North Carolina, Wilmington

Longman

New York   San Francisco   Boston
London   Toronto   Sydney   Tokyo   Singapore   Madrid
Mexico City   Munich   Paris   Cape Town   Hong Kong   Montreal

Acquisitions Editor: Lynn Huddon
Senior Supplements Editor: Donna Campion
Cover Designer: Maria Ilardi Design
Text Design and Electronic Page Makeup: Dianne Hall

Public Literacy, Second Edition, by Elizabeth Ervin

Please visit our Web site at http://www.ablongman.com

ISBN: 0-321-12998-9

345678910—MV—050403

For Don and Willa,
my most vital public interests

INTRODUCTION

As the writing teacher Peter Elbow once said, "life is long and college is short."[1] The purpose of this book is to assist you in doing the kind of writing you are likely to do throughout your life, beyond school and work: public writing.

Public writing can be a way of practicing good citizenship and personal initiative. It can raise awareness about important issues and establish interpersonal relationships. Although it deals with ideas, it concerns itself primarily with action getting things done in the world.

For centuries, learning to use language for public audiences and purposes was central to all levels of schooling. Over the years, though, we have come to value other kinds of writing, and these new priorities have displaced public writing, moving it to the margins of the curriculum under the assumption that it's too controversial or "political" for the classroom and the notion that all writing is essentially the same. This simply isn't true. The need for thoughtful public discourse is as important now as it ever was, but for many people, learning how to engage in it requires a shift in thinking about the purposes and possibilities of writing—new skills and new habits of paying attention.

As a means of fostering these new habits, this book introduces you to a simple but important tool that can help you to recognize and record opportunities to participate in public literacy. This tool is a writer's notebook, and we will make use of it in exercises throughout this book. A writer's notebook is more than just a diary that you use to chronicle the events in your life. Rather, it's a place to collect bits and pieces of information—newspaper clippings, interesting graffiti, gossip, quotations—that may eventually lead to larger writing projects.

The point of a writer's notebook is to help you to become more curious about the world around you and more aware of the myriad opportunities for writing that exist everywhere. Keeping a writer's notebook is a way of being ready to write at any time and never being at a loss for something to write about. Although your teacher might want to look at your writer's notebook from time to time (perhaps to read over your exercises), the notebook is mainly for your use. Therefore, you should use it to record what *you* think is interesting and important, even if it seems silly or insignificant at first.

What you use for your writer's notebook is completely up to you. You can purchase a cloth-bound book with an attractive cover if you like, but a spiral notebook, a sketch-book, a tablet, or just an old folder with paper in it will do just fine. The important thing isn't what your notebook looks like but how you use it. It should be convenient enough to carry around with you in a purse or book bag so that when the inspiration for writing hits or the right opportunity strikes, you'll be ready.

Although you will probably be using this guide as a required textbook for school, you can make your public literacy efforts more meaningful if you see them as advancing your life goals as well as your academic goals. This book will introduce you to a wide variety of people—including many students—whose lives have been improved and en-riched by public writing. Hopefully, their efforts will persuade you that public writing can be a means of changing the world for the better, one word at a time.

Notes

1. Elbow, Peter. "Reflections on Academic Discourse: How It Relates to Freshmen and Colleagues." *College English* 53 (1991): 135–55.

CHAPTER I

What is Public Literacy?

To think about "public literacy" is to plunge into a series of questions that have preoccupied readers, writers, thinkers, and citizens for centuries: How should we define "literacy"? Who, what, and where is "the public"? What does it mean to be literate "in public," or to be a "literate member of the public"? How does "public literacy" differ from other kinds of literacy?

There are many ways to think about these questions, and this guide will not offer definitive answers. Instead, its goals are to help you to become more sophisticated about what public literacy is so that you can be more effective at writing for public audiences and public purposes. As we work toward these goals, we will use several special terms:

Public sphere refers to geographical, textual, or technological sites and forums that are accessible to people (usually at no expense), invite their participation, and provide opportunities for that participation. Examples include sidewalks, public libraries, city council meetings, and the Internet.

Public discourse describes oral, written, and visual utterances that appear in a public sphere. Examples include community radio broadcasts, web pages, political debates, and advertising.

Public literacy designates written language, including written language that is read aloud, that appears in a public sphere and deals with issues of concern to a group of people. Bumper stickers, newspapers, tax forms, and petitions are all examples of public literacy.

Defining Public Literacy: Five Dilemmas

I. The Public and the Civic

In recent years, we've heard a lot about the supposed "deterioration" of public discourse or the "shrinking" of the public sphere. Public debate has been characterized as "the politics of personal destruction," and walls have been erected around whole communities. Critics point out that voter turnout is at an all-time low, and more and more of us are declining to get involved in everything from Boy Scouts to bowling leagues.[1]

While you might agree with this assessment, the fact of the matter is that public discourse is flourishing, thanks in part to mass media outlets like cable television and the World Wide Web. Still, it's hard to argue that tabloid newspapers and Internet pornography are just as good for democracy as neighborliness and informed public debate—which is why it's important to distinguish between *public* discourse and *civic* discourse.

Public discourse has been equated with civic discourse since the Greeks conceptualized a public sphere more than 2500 years ago. Back then, few people knew how to write, so issues were debated, legal decisions were made, and events and people were celebrated or condemned visually (through art and architecture) and orally, through music and rhetoric—a discipline which encompassed philosophy, literature, politics, oratory, and linguistics. The public sphere was literally a place, or rather several places, including markets, theaters, courts, and shrines. Because all citizens were expected to participate in public debate and decision making—and because their livelihoods and status within the community often depended on their effectiveness as speakers—they regularly consulted professional rhetoric teachers. The instructor who assigned this textbook is likely a modern version of those ancient teachers of rhetoric.

During the classical period, rhetoric was practically synonymous with public discourse. Even those texts that were written down—and that we might now enjoy privately or study in solitude, such as poetry or philosophy—were performed orally and discussed with others. Likewise, public discourse was practically synonymous with civic discourse: speech and writing that assisted in the workings of the government. In ancient Greek states like Athens, sports and the arts were enjoyed as entertainment, but like law and education, they were also considered vital to the development and circulation of a national culture and thus served an important civic function as well.

These attitudes continued for centuries and were integral to the development of educational curricula. Although many of us now believe that the primary purpose of a college education is to prepare students to be successful professionals, this wasn't always the case. Until recently, college served as a "training ground" for active citizens and community leaders; rhetoric, literature, philosophy, and other disciplines were studied principally for their applications to public affairs. American universities forged connections to the public life of their communities in a variety of ways. At Harvard University in the eighteenth century, for example, this objective was formalized through such practices as "sitting solstices": oral examinations in which students' performances were evaluated not by their teachers but by fellow citizens.[2] In the early decades of the twentieth century, college writing students were trained as "professional communicators" whose job was to research important issues and events in order to inform citizens—particularly those with little education—of the best means of judging and acting on them.[3]

Because of their long association, many people still perceive public and civic discourse to be the same thing—that is, they believe that all discourse that happens "in public" and purports to engage with "public" issues contributes to civil society. Many factors have ruptured this connection, however, including the complexity and diversity of American culture and the changing role of higher education.

2. One Public or Many?

The population of ancient Athens was relatively small (fewer than 10,000 people), and "citizens" were a pretty homogeneous group: free, white, educated, middle class men. Because they shared similar cultural backgrounds, it was reasonable to assume that participants in the public sphere generally held the same beliefs and values, even if they sometimes disagreed.

This notion of a unified public sphere where everyone shares the same fundamental values has prevailed for centuries and was a central component of eighteenth-century politics and philosophy. It was during this time that the United States formed an independent government and began to develop its own civic values, one of which was that anyone could have access to civic life, including public discourse, if he were smart enough, reasonable enough, and eloquent enough. Conversely, lack of reason and eloquence were presumed to be the only things preventing participation in public discourse—a myth that has been used to justify the exclusion of women, racial and ethnic minorities, immigrants, and the poor from such activities.

The turn-of-the-millennium American public is a much different setting, and yet our ideas about public discourse have been slow to change. To lament the "decline" of public discourse is to suggest that the public sphere continues to be that stable, unified place the Greeks imagined, but that no one is taking advantage of it. In fact, public spheres have never really been stable and unified. The difference now is that we can no longer assume that there is a "general public" where people share the same basic values, religious beliefs, ethnic culture, or even language. Rather, we have many diverse publics. Sometimes these publics overlap or find common ground, but often they come into conflict.

Despite their diversity, publics are more than simply scattered individuals. Members of a public sphere might not know each other personally, but they are aware of themselves as part of a larger organism and often claim a strong group identity. For example, members of the "voting public" don't know all other voters, but they're aware that there *are* other voters and that, among other things, those voters are at least 18 years old.

Even if it is no longer possible to take for granted that all Americans share the same beliefs, values, and cultural backgrounds, it is still possible for most of us to participate in and influence public discourse. Doing so, however, requires that we recognize multiple publics with diverse interests, and that we make an effort to understand the perspectives of these other publics as well as their literacy practices.

3. The Proliferation of Publishing Outlets

Plato, a philosopher from the fifth century BCE, believed that writing would make us lazy and forgetful, a fate which would weaken our ties to each other and, in turn, our commitment to democratic government. There might be some truth to this ancient theory; in fact, some people have made similar claims about the more recent technology of computers. But Plato also cautioned us that writing had the potential to democratize the public sphere, which we now recognize as one of the greatest benefits of writing.

The ability to read, write, and participate in public life hasn't always been democratic in the way we understand that concept today. Indeed, these were once considered privileges reserved for the wealthy, since books, paper, and writing utensils were expensive and few people could afford to attend school. But several phenomena have changed this situation. One is public schooling, which has made literacy education available to a wide variety of people, including non-citizens. Another is the Civil Rights movement, which has empowered non-elite members of our society to take a more active role in local and national affairs—for example, by using newspapers, political campaigns, and websites to inform each other publicly about issues that concern them.

Because the residents of the United States are so diverse, we are interested in and concerned about a broad spectrum of issues. And because so many of us are able to read and write, we have demanded—and created—a variety of forums for reporting and debating these issues, that is, a variety of spheres in which to *publish*, or make available to a public, our ideas. Sometimes these efforts are designed to "speak to" people who already share our perspectives (as with newsletters sent to supporters of a charitable organization). Other times they are designed to reach out to other groups and encourage mutual tolerance, understanding, and cooperation (as with ethnic festivals and some letters to the editor published in newspapers).

The mass media—specifically, advertising and journalism—are important and pervasive sources of public discourse in the United States, in part because our constitution guarantees freedom of the press and in part because we have a capitalist economy. In general, though, participation in these forms of public discourse is limited to trained professionals, not members of the lay public. This textbook is primarily concerned with forms of public literacy that non-professionals and non-experts can effectively participate in and so will not emphasize journalism and advertising.

Exercise

Over the next few days, carry your writer's notebook around your campus, neighborhood, or city. Write down as many different *public spheres* as you can find: places or forums in which people publish opinions, ideas, and information. These may include newspapers, television channels, newsletters, bulletin boards, community centers, websites, and local events; you should be able to identify many more. As you record your observations, think about how and why these public spheres differ in format and location, as well as the kinds of interests, concerns, or populations they represent.

4. The Public Interest

Because there are now so many places to publish our ideas, it is becoming increasingly difficult to determine who profits from public discourse. Let's take as an example a recent series of multimedia public service announcements (PSAs) sponsored by an organization called "truth," whose mission is to expose the business practices of tobacco companies and the health risks of smoking. One of the PSAs features the truth squad sticking little signs into piles of dog waste. Fashioned out of paper and drinking straws, these signs creatively call attention to the fact that tobacco companies add ammonia to cigarettes.[4]

Certainly, many people would agree that reducing tobacco addiction among young people is indeed a matter of *public interest*—of relevance or concern to a broad cross-section of people—whether for ethical, medical, or other reasons. But when we consider that truth is funded by the American Legacy Foundation, an organization established by tobacco companies in 1998 as part of a major lawsuit settlement, it's also possible to question the group's motives. Is the tobacco industry sponsoring the truth campaign because they are genuinely concerned about teen smoking or because they might benefit from *publicity*—public attention—for their in-your-face PSAs? How much "truth" are they telling and how much are they leaving out?

To be fair, truth has *publicized*—brought to public attention—many unsavory facts about the tobacco industry, tobacco marketing, and tobacco use. But the point is that it's not always easy to distinguish personal interest from public interest. Is an organization called "Americans for Hope, Growth, and Opportunity" really concerned with promoting economic security for all Americans, as its name suggests, or is it mainly concerned with preserving tax breaks for a small group of wealthy individuals? Do politicians really care about improving their constituents' quality of life, or are they simply seeking fame or personal gain? In other words, who benefits from public discourse?

This question is trickier than it might initially appear. Sometimes, of course, private interests are clearly at odds with public interests. For example, if a politician introduced legislation written in such a way that it would *only* benefit him or one of his associates, this would represent an obvious conflict of interest.

Often, however, self interests are compatible with public interests. On a typical college campus, for instance, you are likely to see flyers selling everything from French tutoring sessions to surf boards and seeking everything from a roommate to a ride home. While these flyers are self-interested in that they are designed to benefit individual people, they also serve the public interest by contributing to the sense that the campus is a community whose members can appeal to each other for assistance and mutual support—financial, social, and intellectual.

Another difficulty in determining public interest is the fact that *public* is often defined as the opposite of *private*. This distinction is misleading. Domestic violence was regarded as a private matter in the United States until fairly recently because it usually occurred in family residences (some Americans still consider it private, as do members of many cultures throughout the world). Consequently, it was not deemed appropriate or necessary to make laws or devote public resources to preventing domestic violence, punishing its perpetrators, or assisting its victims. Eventually it became clear that issues deemed "private" have a disproportionate effect on women and children, many of whom spend more time at home. In the 1960s, feminists coined the phrase "the personal is political" to draw attention to the fact that things that happen "in private" often have public significance.

The inverse of this phenomenon is also true; that is, private information can be more public than we realize. Some personal information—including births and deaths, home addresses and phone numbers, and court decisions—is regarded as so important to the public interest that it is published in newspapers and community directories without anyone's formal permission. Most Americans understand and accept this practice. However, many people are surprised to learn that their credit ratings, e-mail addresses, and spending habits can also be published and even sold. Sometimes the privacy of this information can be maintained only when consumers submit written requests. While this may be disturbing, the fact is that most people volunteer this information without a second thought—for example, when we wish to access certain websites or when the cashier at our favorite store asks for our zip code.

5. Public Domain

Although it sounds like a synonym for public sphere, in actuality public domain refers to who "owns" knowledge, information, ideas, art, and natural resources: the public or private individuals? In other words, when is information freely usable by all and when is it necessary to give credit, obtain permission, or pay a fee in order to use it? Answers to these questions have always been complex, requiring an understanding of arcane patent and copyright laws, licensing agreements, and so on. In recent years, however, technological advancements have made the issues even more difficult to sort through. The Internet music-sharing site Napster stepped right into the middle of these legal, ethical, and intellectual dilemmas when it began making music available for downloading on the World Wide Web in 2000.

At issue is what constitutes *intellectual property*. Legally, it can be virtually anything that a person creates, including ideas, songs, scientific formulas, and inventions. Most of us want to reap the benefits of our original productions—financial or otherwise—which means that we want to own and control our intellectual property (and which is why so many musicians oppose Internet sites like Napster).

The public domain is a space where intellectual property protection does not apply. Sometimes, information and creative works fall into the public domain after a certain amount of time (e.g., when a patent expires). And some people believe so strongly that access to information and art encourages intellectual and democratic discernment that they voluntarily contribute their intellectual property to the public domain. In doing so, they may waive their copyrights, encourage people to share their work with others (as with "shareware" software, for example), and even grant permission for others to use their work without acknowledgment.[5]

These people are the exceptions, however. Most information that is accessible via a public sphere, including the Internet, is *not* part of the public domain. Therefore, it must be as meticulously documented in your research as a book or article you found at the library. Unfortunately, it's not uncommon to find materials on the Web that are obviously "fishy" (e.g., term papers for sale); it's also not uncommon to find materials with crucial information missing (e.g., the publication date). Still, unless the author grants you explicit written permission to use his work without acknowledgment, it is your responsibility as a writer to thoroughly and accurately document every source you use. *Failure to do so constitutes plagiarism*; this is one of the most serious ethical breaches a writer can make, and the consequences are equally serious. If you're not sure how to document electronic (or other) source materials, ask your teacher to recommend an appropriate handbook.

Just because information is legitimately part of the public domain does not mean that it is easily accessible. The federal government, in particular, has historically been reluctant to disclose documents that might reveal its employees (including elected officials) to be unethical or incompetent. In 1966, however, Congress passed the Freedom of Information Act (FOIA), which created procedures whereby any member of the public may obtain records of any federal agency. Of course, government officials are still resisting the FOIA, often claiming that requested information is exempted. Such efforts to shrink the public sphere remind us yet again why public writing—filing an FOIA request, for instance—remains so vital to the interests of a democracy.

Exercise

Several organizations provide detailed information on how the FOIA works, what it does and does not cover, and how to file a request. One is the American Civil Liberties Union, whose website (*http://www.aclu.org/library/foia.html*) offers extensive advice, including sample letters and appeal procedures. Another, the Reporters Committee for Freedom of the Press (*http://www.rcfp.org/foi_lett.html*), even furnishes a fill-in-the-blank form to assist you in composing your letter (it also staffs a 24-hour hotline for FOIA-related questions).

Visit the website for the ACLU or the RCFP and file an FOIA request—either for a legitimate purpose such as a research project or just for the experience.

(Keep in mind that you might have to pay photocopying and postage expenses.) Does the CIA have a file on you? Find out courtesy of the FOIA.

CASE IN POINT: CONFLICT OF INTEREST

In 2001, President George W. Bush established a task force to draft a national energy policy. Headed by Vice President Dick Cheney, himself a former oil company executive, the final report of the Energy Task Force recommended increased domestic energy production, deregulation of energy markets, and tax breaks for industries such as gas and coal without comparable incentives for energy conservation and the development of renewable energy technologies such as wind and solar power. Perhaps most controversially, the report advocated drilling in Alaska's Arctic National Wildlife Refuge as a way for the United States to reduce its dependency on foreign oil.

Concerns about these proposals intensified when news reports alleged that members of the Task Force had met privately with energy industry lobbyists and campaign contributors to discuss and even write the energy policy. In response to these charges, the General Accounting Office (GAO)—the nonpartisan investigative arm of Congress—requested that Vice President Cheney submit documents related to the Task Force's operations and staff. The Vice President refused, arguing that such a request represented an unconstitutional interference in the functioning of the executive branch of the federal government. In 2002, under threat of legal action, the Department of Energy provided the requested documents to the GAO, but information was deleted from some pages and other pages were missing altogether.

While most citizens and residents of the United States are confident that their government works in the public interest, many believe that the Energy Task Force report exposed a serious conflict of interest. In other words, they believe that although Mr. Cheney acted within his authority as an elected public official charged with establishing a national policy agenda, his recommendations benefited a small number of his associates at the expense of most American taxpayers. What do you think?

Alone or in small groups, do some research on this controversy. The following Internet sites provide useful information from a variety of perspectives that purport to represent the public interest, including the White House itself. Read the relevant sections of these sites and follow any links that seem interesting. (Since some of the sites represent "clearinghouses," with links to related sites and news items, you may notice some overlap.)

Reports by the Center for Public Integrity (search "cheney energy task force"):
> http://www.publicintegrity.org/dtaweb/home.asp

Documents collected by the Environmental Media Service:
> http://www.ems.org/energy_policy/cheney_energy_task_force.html

Documents from the U.S. House of Representatives Committee on Government Reform, including GAO reports and correspondence:

> http://www.house.gov/reform/min/inves_energy/index.htm

Statements by the White House:

> http://www.whitehouse.gov/infocus/energy/

Department of Energy documents released to the GAO and obtained by other groups such as the Natural Resources Defense Council:

> http://www.nrdc.org/air/energy/taskforce/tfinx.asp

As you do your research, think about the following questions:

- How do the goals of the various organizations or institutions affect the ways in which they understand the concept of "public interest"? (Many organizations publish a mission statement, usually on their website's home page; if you can't find one, try to infer a group's goals from the content of its website.) Having explored their sites, are you convinced that all of these organizations or institutions do, in their own ways, represent the public interest? Why or why not?

- What different forms of writing have been used to discuss and publicize this issue? Why do you think writers have chosen to use so many genres to make sense of and publicize the same information?

If the recommended sites are no longer active, use a database like EBSCOhost or Lexis-Nexis to find some newspaper and magazine articles that deal with the controversy. Or, if you prefer, use the same strategies to investigate a different issue altogether. Since it's not uncommon for politicians to be accused of conflicts of interest, you will probably have many issues to choose from.

SO WHAT?

With all this complexity and confusion over what counts as a public issue, you might be wondering why it matters whether something can be defined as "public." There are several reasons, including helping you to:

- set priorities about what problems or issues are most important to you and thus which ones to devote your energy and attention to;

- determine how decisions are made and thus what problems or issues you can effectively influence through writing;

- identify like-minded people who might join you in building coalitions and support you in your efforts to write for public audiences and purposes; and

- discover or create opportunities to participate in public discourse at school or your workplace.

Of course, the most important decision is whether or not to participate in public discourse in the first place. As the saying goes, "If you stand for nothing you'll fall for anything." In other words, if you don't make an effort to understand and form opinions about public issues, then you're at the mercy of the people who *are* willing to make that effort—people who may not have the public's interests at heart.

Exercise

In your notebook, take a few minutes to generate a list of issues that interest or concern you personally. These may include social or political causes that matter a lot to you, or simply problems or events that are on your mind. Then, in small groups, discuss ways in which your interests and concerns might have public significance. You might want to generate a list of organizations whose agendas are consistent with your interests (if you know of any) or public spheres where you could "publish" your concerns.

Once you've identified ways in which your interests are also public interests, you can begin to focus your attention on discussions of those issues, keeping an eye and ear out for opportunities to contribute to them as you read the newspaper, walk to school, talk with friends, and so on. There might be meetings, public lectures, fund-raisers, or other events or projects related to your interests that you could participate in—or better yet, whose efforts you could assist by contributing your writing skills and rhetorical knowledge.

Tracy Nazarchyk is a first-generation college student from Charlotte, North Carolina. Tracy is studying English with the goal of teaching or working with community literacy programs; since her grandfather died of cancer last year, she has a special interest in hospice care, and is curious about the uses of writing among elderly and critically ill populations. Tracy is currently employed as a restaurant hostess and also has concerns about the working conditions there. Her sole experience with public literacy involved writing to a cereal company to complain about a change in her favorite breakfast food.

Tracy's list:

Will my car make it past 90,000 miles?

Why is the water evaporating out of my fish tank?

I had $150 and just paid $60 in bills.

Hurricane season starts next month.

Will my insurance cover hospital tests on Monday?

I worry if people recycle the Domino's flyers and how it is an invasion of my privacy to put them on the door because we have signs that say NO SOLICITING.

I worry about all the new buildings on campus where there used to be grass and trees (and community development too).

pesticides on vegetables in the grocery store

We are not very handicap accessible at work.

traffic: too many people run red lights and speed

The local newspaper lists "bride of . . ." exclusively in its wedding announcements.

On TV the latest Survivor "winner" described herself as a Christian and then related her deceitful, manipulative, fraud-against-her-fellow-human-beings tactics to "win."

I know a woman my age diagnosed with cancer.

Not all of the items on Tracy's list have public significance—the mysterious problem with her fish tank, for example. But many of her personal concerns—such as health care, food safety, and disability rights—are issues that lots of people care about. Other issues, such as the large amount of her paycheck going toward bills, could be seen as part of broader conversations about taxes or the minimum wage.

When Tracy shared her list with a small group of classmates, one of them told her about a local food co-op that sells organic produce and publishes a newsletter written by and for members. Another mentioned that the campus Environmental Concerns Organization (ECO) might share her anxieties about the environmental impact of new buildings on campus.

Sometimes it can be hard for one person to make a difference in big public issues, but these suggestions illustrate how we can assist each other in finding strength in numbers. As Margaret Mead once put it, "Never doubt that a small group of thoughtful, committed citizens can change the world; indeed, it's the only thing that ever does."

Notes

1. Putnam, Robert D. "Bowling Alone: America's Declining Social Capital." *Journal of Democracy* 6 (1995): 65–78.

2. Halloran, S. Michael, "Rhetoric in the American College Curriculum: The Decline of Public Discourse." (*PRE/TEXT* 3.3 [1982]: 245–69).

3. Adams, Katherine H. *Progressive Politics and the Training of America's Persuaders.* Mahway, NJ: LEA, 1999.

4. *Truth.* July 2002 <http://www.thetruth.com>.

5. *Center for the Public Domain.* July 2002. <http://www.centerforthepublicdomain.org>.

CHAPTER 2

Four Configurations of the Public Sphere

You've probably heard the terms "general public" or "average Americans" to describe people who have graduated from high school, speak English, read the newspaper, work outside the home, drive, take vacations, and so on. This description might even fit you. But what about the millions of people in this country who don't know how to read, don't have a stable job or residence, can't afford a car or a college education, and don't identify themselves as "American"? When we start to think about how many people are excluded from commonly held definitions of the "general public," it becomes clear that there's no such thing.

The myth of a general public is a remnant of the idea that there is a unified public sphere to which everyone has equal access. But as we discussed in Chapter 1, there are many public spheres, owing to a diverse population with varied public interests. And although there is considerable overlap among these public spheres—and many exceptions to the ways we might define them—it is possible to identify distinct purposes, locations, and literacy practices for each.

I. The National Public

There might not be any such thing as an "average" American, but there is something that all of us—even those who are not citizens—have in common: we are equally protected by the laws of this country and equally responsible for obeying them. Unfortunately, there have been many situations in which laws have been applied unequally and people have received more or less than their fair share of justice, often because of their race or economic status. But it is because of these situations that public discourse continues to be important: if we perceive injustices, we have the right—some would say the responsibility—to speak out against them and enact positive changes. Writing is a tool that can assist us with such efforts.

This guide will use the term *national public* to describe the vast and diverse group of people who live within the geographical boundaries of a given country and citizens of that country who live abroad—military service personnel, for instance. The national public has its roots in public institutions (such as government, schools, and some mass media) and formal organizations (such as workplaces and agencies), all of which engage in different kinds of literacy activities.

In the United States, written documents that deal with laws, rights, and policies of the federal government are examples of national public literacies. Other examples include widely used public school textbooks, materials distributed by government or nonprofit agencies, national moneys, postage stamps, and some newspapers. Because not all residents of the United States speak English, and because laws, rights, and information about government services apply to everyone, these texts may appear in a variety of languages.

Of course, the United States isn't the only country with a national public sphere. All countries have them, and the public literacies of any national public inevitably reflect the values of that government. Let's take as a simple example national moneys. In the United States, all bank notes and coins feature the words *"e pluribus unum"*—"from many, one"—and include likenesses of famous national monuments and, usually, former presidents; these words and images reflect this country's professed commitment to freedom and equality for a diverse citizenry, as well as its reverence for national symbols. Equally importantly, these objects represent the same amount of money for everyone—a dollar equals a dollar whether you're a stock broker on Wall Street or a Hmong immigrant in Merced, California.

Canadian money also memorializes important political figures but eschews mottoes and monuments. For example, the front of the Canadian five dollar bill features former Prime Minister Wilfrid Laurie, while the back depicts children engaged in various winter sports and includes a quotation, translated in both English and French, from Canadian writer and National Librarian Roch Carrier: "The winters of my childhood were long, long seasons. We lived in three places—the school, the church and the skating-rink—but our real life was on the skating rink." Combined, the bilingual text and the iconography reveal a different national culture as well as a different national monetary system.

Figure 2.1. National public literacy texts like currency and postage stamps are so ubiquitous that we may take them for granted, but as the back of this Canadian five dollar bill illustrates, they can reveal much about the "official" values of a government.

http://aes.iupui.edu/rwise/default.htm

Sometimes national public literacies amount to *propaganda*: extremely biased messages that are directed toward mass audiences in order to influence them to support special interests, especially government policies. Propaganda messages are pervasive and often show up in seemingly "neutral" settings. At the Homa Hotel in Teheran, Iran, for example, the message "Down With U.S.A." is tiled into the wall above the front door of the lobby; the fact that the message appears in English rather than Arabic is significant and will be discussed in more detail in this chapter's section on "Global Rhetorics."[1]

When United States military forces invaded Afghanistan in 2001, there was much concern that Arab nations would view our actions as an attack on Islam rather than an attack on the Taliban government. In an effort to gain the support of the Afghan people, the United States initiated a comprehensive propaganda campaign assuring Afghan citizens of our good intentions. Some of these messages took the form of leaflets dropped from airplanes. One example shows an American soldier extending his hand to an Afghan man in traditional dress and the words "The Partnership of Nations is here to help" on the front and "The Partnership of Nations is here to assist the People of Afghanistan" on the back. Although writers of the leaflets produced several versions written in different languages spoken in Afghanistan, they failed to consider that most Afghan people are uneducated and illiterate. Thus the leaflets—widely publicized in the United States—may have been more effective in rallying American support for the war and for the United States government.

Figure 2.2. National public literacy documents like these 2001 propaganda leaflets were designed to gain support and goodwill from a variety of people affected by American military actions in Afghanistan.[2]

http://www.psywarrior.com/afghanleaf.html

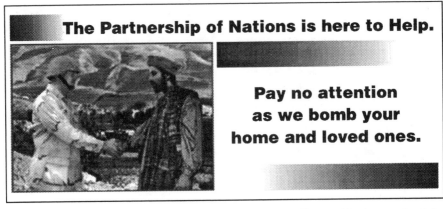

Figure 2.3. Some people remained dubious of the war effort, as illustrated by this parody of the propaganda leaflets.[3]

http://yorick.infinitejest.org:81/1/afghanistan_leaflets.html

2. Local Publics

People often decline to participate in public literacy because "public issues" seem remote from their lives. It's true that if you read the *Christian Science Monitor* or watch the evening news, the focus is often on national or international events that seem far away or on huge social problems like AIDS or drug trafficking that seem so abstract that it's hard to believe one person could alter their course. In reality, though, these issues often have a profound impact on our lives, and within our local communities one person can directly influence the nature of this impact.

In this book, we will use the term *local publics* to describe those people and institutions that are influenced by specific geographical locations, histories, traditions, cultures, values, and dialects. Local publics may translate national issues into specific contexts, prioritize them differently than national publics do, or ignore them altogether; they may also have unique concerns that do not affect people who live elsewhere. Local publics may be defined narrowly (e.g., as a neighborhood, borough, or city) or broadly (as a county, state, or region) and offer specific opportunities and challenges for participating in public literacy.

Examples of local public literacies include state and local laws, ordinances, or procedures; promotional information for local events; and newspapers with primarily state, local, or regional readerships. Like their counterparts on the national level, local public literacies reflect the interests and values of a specific community. Bloomington, Illinois, for example, is like most towns in that it renounces racism. But Bloomington makes this value "official" by making racial tolerance a part of its local public discourse—specifically, by posting signs that say "Not in Our Town—No Racism" at every entrance to the city and on every municipal vehicle.

Local literacies might appear in a variety of languages and be written from highly specific cultural perspectives. For example, in New York City neighborhoods with large populations of Eastern European Jews, automatic teller machines offer instructions in Yiddish, a Hebrew dialect, as well as in English. In cities like Portland, Oregon, it is not uncommon to find a newspaper such as *These Homeless Times*, which is written entirely by the homeless and formerly homeless; although oriented specifically to the experiences and concerns of homeless people, publications like this are available (usually for a donation) to all interested readers.

Believe it or not, some local communities—like Ithaca, New York—actually have their own currencies. "Ithaca Hours" are locally printed, accepted along with United States dollars and cents at over 300 businesses in that community, and used to fund grants and interest-free loans for members of the local public. Since Ithaca Hours represent taxable income, some people even accept them as part of their wages. Participants in the program are listed in a weekly newspaper, *Hour Town*. While citizens of Ithaca aren't required to "buy into" this alternative economic system, the fact that it exists at all, and that it is supported by many layers of local literacy texts, suggests something about the values of that community—as well as its relationship to national institutions.

Figure 2.4. Some communities print their own money depicting local landmarks, honored citizens, and slogans. These documents reinterpret national public literacies to fit local needs and priorities.

http://www.ithacahours.com/currency.html

Exercise

Visitors to the Church Street Marketplace in Burlington, Vermont, can relax next to a fountain that bears the following sign:

> This is a lovely spot to think,
> but not a place to take a drink.
>
> It's great for making dreamy wishes,
> but not for swimming like the fishes.
>
> Go on—dunk a wriggling toe or two!
> (But not a headful of shampoo.)
>
> And if you feel the urge to spout,
> make sure it's poetry coming out.

If it's true that local public literacies say something about the communities in which they are located, what can you infer about Burlington from this sign? What kinds of people live there and what do they value? Why do you think city representatives chose to post a sign like this one rather than something more efficient and authoritative like "No Swimming" or a bottle of shampoo with a big red "no" symbol drawn through it?

After you have discussed these questions in small groups, make a list of several signs you have seen in your own local community (you might have already recorded some examples in your writer's notebook). Then, rewrite the signs with a different local public in mind. Be as specific as possible, and consider familiar publics (e.g., dormitory residents on your campus) as well as unfamiliar ones (e.g., an affluent retirement neighborhood), very homogeneous publics (e.g., a Mormon village in Utah) as well as very diverse ones (e.g., visitors to a national park).

3. Global Publics

The concept of globalism has been around for as long as countries have traded with their neighbors and sent explorers out to find new territory. Its current manifestation is an economic and political philosophy promoted by multinational corporations and their government supporters, who believe that unregulated corporate expansion creates a more efficient free market, which in turn promises greater economic prosperity, political stability, and international cooperation for people around the world. Opponents of globalism, however—which include conservationists, labor unions, and many religious groups—point to corporations like McDonald's, Starbucks, and AOL Time Warner as evidence that cheaper, more plentiful consumer goods come at a price: environmental degradation, human rights abuses, cultural imperialism, and restricted flow of information. Protests at meetings of the International Monetary Fund and World Bank represent the clash of these ideologies.

In some ways, *global publics* blend characteristics of national and local publics. In fact, some people ominously refer to globalism as "world nationalism," while others speak blissfully of a "global village" in which local cultures are preserved but made more accessible to people everywhere through technology and diplomacy (think Disney World's Epcot Center). Unlike national and local publics, however, global publics are not restricted by geographical boundaries, laws, or even languages. Rather, they are governed by international treaties like the North American Free Trade Agreement (NAFTA) and organizations like the World Trade Organization (WTO).

Global public literacies use language strategically to participate in global conversations. For the purposes of this textbook, what makes these conversations "global" is not so much their subject matter but the fact that when they occur publicly, they frequently occur in English—as with the anti-American sentiments embellishing the Iranian hotel. Why English? One reason is that the messages are often intended for Americans, who can influence U.S. foreign policy and public opinion on the writers' behalf. Many governments actually print their national moneys in English as well as in their native language(s), even when English is not normally spoken or written by that country's citizens, in an effort to appeal to powerful corporate interests in the United States as well as individual American consumers.

In 1952 a coalition of European nations began an experiment in globalism that eventually evolved into the European Union (E.U.). Although each member nation still enjoys its own national government, the E.U. has established a host of transnational agencies and in 1999 introduced its own money, the euro. This centralized economic system effectively erases the cultural specificity of national currencies—French people no longer use francs, for example. However, the E.U. has attempted to respect national languages and symbols in its design of this new money. For one thing, all writing on the euro appears in five linguistic variants, representing the 11 official languages of the European Community. For another, euro coins feature both a common side and a country-specific side, while banknotes depict bridges—symbolic of openness, cooperation, and harmony among European nations and the rest of the world.

Figure 2.5–2.6. One side of this Euro 2 features a map of Europe; the other depicts an eagle, a traditional symbol of German sovereignty, and the German national motto *"einigket und recht und freiheit"* ("unity, justice and freedom"). The tensions between national identity and transnational authority typify the complexities of public literacy in a global context.

http://www.euro.ecb.int/ en/section/euro0/coins.html

http://www.euro.ecb.int/en/ section/euro0/specific.DE.html

4. Everyday Publics

Not all public literacies are related to politics or solemn public issues, of course. Sometimes people use public literacy simply to have fun, share information, or build relationships. In a college dormitory, you are likely to see personal messages on doors, flyers posted in the stairwell announcing social events, and bulletin boards in the lounge documenting residents' life together. Your roommate's guacamole recipe, directions to a nightclub across town, or someone's physics notes might also be floating around. These texts can all be examples of public literacy.

Everyday publics describe people in their interpersonal relationships or informal social and political networks.[4] They may be geographically specific (e.g., invitations to a neighborhood block party), but they don't have to be (e.g., holiday newsletters that update friends and relatives about the year's events). Everyday public literacies have their roots in ordinary human experiences rather than dominant social institutions such as law, education, government, and the workplace. Because they are "unofficial" documents, they are not regulated by the formal rules, procedures, and literacy practices of these institutions, although they may be influenced by them.

Everyday public literacies tend to be quite relaxed; words might be scribbled on a napkin, with little attention to neatness or correctness, because those conventions simply aren't important to all people all the time. After a hurricane hit Wilmington, North Carolina, in 1999, a hand-painted sign appeared alongside the road that read "Hurican Debre" and included an arrow and a hurricane symbol: ↺ . Despite the misspellings, the workers who were collecting hurricane debris probably found the pile easily.

Often, everyday literacy texts imitate the format, language, and overall appearance of "official" literacies in order to establish credibility or authority within other public spheres, as when a special interest group circulates a petition to present to the City Council. Sometimes, though, writers may adopt dominant literacy practices in order to critique national, local, and global institutions. Consider a flyer that was posted in the Capitol Hill neighborhood of Washington, DC, by a residents group who complained that police were ignoring their reports of violence and drug dealing. At first glance, the flyer looks like a professionally designed event promotion: it includes addresses, "trademarks," and even "reviews" from the *Washington Post*. At second glance, however, it becomes clear that the flyer isn't what it appears.

The Crack Cocaine Dealers of Capitol Hill® want to

Rock Your World

We operate convenient, full-service outlets and guarantee no police hassles or interference.

Stop by and talk to our sales associates at:

1300 block of D Street SE
(Convenient for Safeway shoppers.)
1600 block C Street SE
(Right behind a Metropolitan Boys and Girls Club.)
16th and D Streets
(Just pull over, roll down your window.)
16th and E Street
(New locale! Excellent for late-night needs.)
300 block 14th Street
(Conveniently located behind a liquor store. Always a party!)

WE ACCEPT CASH OR STOLEN GOODS.

Coming Soon: The annual Capitol Hill Crack House & Alley Tour®. See functioning drug dens, meet dysfunctional crackheads. Visit 232 14th Street, the house where Officer Jason White was killed, and other locales on 14th, 15th, 16th and E Streets SE where crack is sold and smoked. The *Post* called it, "a moving experience ... addicts are moving in and residents are moving out ... real estate bargains galore."

Figure 2.7. Everyday public literacy texts are often informal and social in orientation. This flyer, however, not only resembles a professionally designed document but also addresses a serious social issue.[5]

Subversive forms of everyday literacy can be just as effective as national, local, and global literacies—sometimes even more so. In this case, the flyer succeeded in summoning police to the troubled neighborhood within hours of being posted. Perhaps even more importantly, it drew national attention to the lax enforcement of national and local drug laws in the United States capitol. (The flyer was reprinted in *Harper's* magazine.)

Exercise

Separate a page in your writer's notebook into four columns; write *national* at the top of one column, *local* at the top of another, *everyday* at the top of the third, and *global* at the top of the fourth. Then, alone or in small groups, brainstrom examples of each kind of public literacy. Be as specific as possible.

For example, instead of "billboard," write "the billboards that are supposed to be messages from God."

Debbie Asberry is from Dayton, Ohio. In addition to working full time for a pharmaceutical company, she studies photography at a local community college and would like one day to earn a nursing degree. Debbie is also the mother of a young son, and since her husband's work often takes him out of town for several days at a time, she sometimes struggles to fulfill all of her responsibilities. Not surprisingly, Debbie is concerned about day care and children's health issues; in addition, she is interested in the local arts scene and "anything to do with the environment." Debbie has written many consumer complaint letters and has even assisted friends in writing such letters. She also recalls signing various petitions over the years—most recently one against human cloning.

Debbie's lists:

National
Social Security forms

mailings from St. Jude's Ranch for Children (describing programs, etc.)

student loan application

Warren Commission reports

Local
Café Deluxe billboard "Voted favorite restaurant in the Cape Fear region!"

campaign signs for local and state candidates

church marquee—announces upcoming events

schedule of events for Greek festival?

Everyday
note by mailboxes at apartment complex: "Apt. 1104, I got your package by mistake. Call Kristen at 962-3655"

"Congratulations Chris and Tina—Just Married" sign propped up against a tree in someone's yard

"Just Graduated" sign in car window

"ART" spelled out in Christmas lights on roof of house downtown

Global
IMF meetings and protests

Bush's speeches often make international news

proceedings of United Nations laws war crimes tribunal

publications of international relief groups—Amnesty International, Doctors Without Borders, etc.

website for La Leche League International (you can choose from many languages)

Four Public Literacies in Action

Sometimes it might be difficult to distinguish national, local, global, and everyday public literacies from one another or to see how they might influence one another. It might be useful, then, to look at an extended example: political protests.

1. National Public Literacies

The first amendment of the United States Constitution reads:

> Congress shall make no law respecting an establishment of religion, or pro-hibiting the free exercise thereof; or abridging the freedom of speech, or of the press; or the right of the people peaceably to assemble, and to petition the Government for a redress of grievances.

Because this document applies to—and belongs to—all Americans, it is an example of national public literacy. However, because it is also highly ambiguous, it has been in-terpreted in many different ways.

For example, some people believe that burning the American flag represents a legal form of political protest. Others, however, believe that this form of expression repre-sents treason—an illegal offense—and thus support the passage of a Constitutional amendment that explictly bans such actions. The Supreme Court and various lower courts have responded to this confusion by issuing numerous (sometimes contradic-tory) legal decisions attempting to clarify the amendment's meaning, and these deci-sions are likewise national public documents.

2. Local Public Literacies

Most communities require citizens to obtain permits granting them permission to as-semble in public places such as parks, sidewalks, and government buildings. One form of assembly is picketing, which in Wilmington, North Carolina, is regulated by Sec-tions 6-13 and 6-14 of the City Code. Copies of these documents, and of "Notice of Intent to Picket" forms, are available at the local police station. The form must be filled out and approved at least a week before the scheduled event so that the police can notify the appropriate offices (e.g., Traffic Engineering) and provide necessary per-sonnel or equipment (e.g., barricades).

Because the freedom to assemble is guaranteed by the United States Constitution, no community can prohibit public gatherings or punish those who peacefully and lawfully participate in them. However, all municipalities have the right to regulate such activities according to their local needs, traditions, and resources—as long as their policies don't violate other federal laws or rights.

3. Everyday Public Literacies

Everyday publics can sometimes publicize and assemble for events without special permission from the government, even if those events are political in orientation. For example, a neighborhood threatened by the construction of a new road posted hand-lettered signs urging people to attend an informational meeting on the subject. One such sign read:

DON'T LET THEM RUN A HIGHWAY
THROUGH COLLEGE ACRES!

COME TO A PUBLIC HEARING
MARCH 26 @ 7:00
COLLEGE PARK ELEMENTARY

PLEASE BE THERE!!

This sign was carefully edited but obviously written hastily, befitting the urgency of the concern. This public hearing took place in a public building (a school) and was also announced by the local newspaper. Because the event was sponsored by the local government, the person or group who produced this document probably didn't have to apply for any local permits to assemble. The signs, then, represented an unofficial effort to involve neighbors in an official local event of significance to their lives.

Everyday public gatherings that take place at private residences—such as book group meetings and backyard barbecues—need no authorization from the local government. Some neighborhoods or apartment complexes may have common areas—such as club houses or swimming pools—with policies governing their use, but as long as these policies are adhered to, no one can prohibit such peaceful gatherings from taking place.

4. Global Public Literacies

The laws regulating political protests, the documents produced as part of the protests, and the protests themselves represent different forms of public literacy. Freedoms to assemble and to publicly express political opinions vary from country to country, however, which is why some protesters choose to communicate their concerns privately rather than risk political reprisal. In countries where dissenting opinions are not tolerated, texts that criticize the government or deviate from official perspectives may be censored, resulting in a subdued public sphere dominated by propaganda.

Since global public spheres transcend geographical boundaries, public literacies may be regulated by international treaties, proclamations, or other agreements. For example, local or national laws protecting workers' rights or the environment can in some cases be nullified by global treaties that guarantee free trade. In response to such policies, some protesters choose to express their concerns in languages other than their own—often English—and direct them at audiences in the United States, usually through journalists. In doing so, they acknowledge not only that English is widely spoken throughout the world but also that the U.S. government wields enormous political and economic power. Ironically, the United States itself has no national language, so English may be more a global language than a national one.

Exercise

As you carry around your writer's notebook, record as many different examples of public literacy as you can find. If possible, photocopy, photograph, sketch, or even take possession of the documents. (If a document is promoting an upcoming event or is someone else's property, don't take it.) Add these examples to the lists of national, local, and everyday public literacy documents you generated in small groups, and use them for ongoing consultation as you begin to make decisions about how you can participate in public literacy.

In small groups, carefully examine the documents you have found. First, decide whether they represent examples of national, local, global, or everyday public literacies—or some combination of these. Then, using the following questions, begin speculating about the circumstances that invited the production of each text and make preliminary judgments about their purposes and effectiveness.

- Where was the document published (made available to a public)?
- Who wrote it?
- How was the document produced and distributed? What is it written on? How many copies exist?
- What is the document's purpose? What does it seek to accomplish?
- How might you characterize the language and tone of the document?
- What striking or unusual features, if any, do you notice about the document? What is your general impression of its quality?

Case in Point: Parodies

Earlier in this chapter we examined a parody of American propaganda leaflets air-dropped in Afghanistan. Although the message might seem unpatriotic or in poor taste, the fact is that parodies occupy a distinguished place in the history of public literacy. At first glance parodies are likely to make us angry or make us laugh. However, it's not because of their humor that parodies merit serious attention as forms of public literacy: it's because they also offer critiques of dominant political or cultural assumptions. The parody of the Afghanistan leaflets, for example, suggests that the United States's war effort might not have been as noble or as carefully executed as the military wanted people to believe.

But what exactly is a parody? In general, it's a literary or visual text that uses mimicry and exaggeration as a way of holding up to public scrutiny important public figures, public issues, or public texts. All parodies contain enough accurate information to make their subject matter recognizable, but they transform this information in ways that force audiences to think twice about the text's purpose and, in the process, about their own beliefs and perceptions. While most parodies are clearly irreverent, others are so subtle that some audiences might not even realize that they *are* parodies. And while it might be possible to interpret some parodies as complimentary of their subjects, most express dissent and can be instrumental in shaping public opinion.

Recently, a secretive organization called "the Yes Men" gained international attention for their ironically named website *http://www.gatt.org*, which included numerous parodies of the philosophies, policies, and practices of the General Agreement on Tariffs and Trade (GATT) and the World Trade Organization (WTO), two of the most powerful proponents of global economics. The WTO has since gained control of the *gatt* domain (the above URL now takes web browsers to the official WTO website), but the Yes Men can still be found at *http://www.theyesmen.org*.

Alone or in small groups, explore the Yes Men website, following interesting links. Keep the following questions in mind:

- How do you know which of the Yes Men's texts are parodies and which ones aren't? How do you know what information is accurate? Does it matter? Why might a parody writer want readers to question the accuracy of his or her information?

- Why do you think that some audiences have confused the Yes Men's parodies with sincere advocacy of global economics?

- What do you think the Yes Men are trying to accomplish with their parodies? In your opinion, are they effective? Why do you think they use parodies to convey their message rather than more straightforward means of critique? Are some subjects, styles, or authors especially vulnerable to parody?

If the Yes Men's site is no longer active, use a search engine like Google to find paro-dies of some other organization, text, public figure, or icon (there are numerous Bar-bie parody sites, for example) and ask yourself the same questions. You may also wish to consult well-known satirical publications like *The Onion*, which can be found on-line at *www.theonion.com*, or webzines like *http://www.infinitejest.org*. Many political cartoonists make use of parody; *This Modern World* by Tom Tomorrow is one that can be found online at *http://www.thismodernworld.com*, and others can be found in virtu-ally any newspaper.

Once you have looked at several examples of parodies, you might want to attempt to write or draw one of your own. Start by choosing a target; then identify which features of that target might be most sensitive to critique. Being sarcastic or even insulting comes easy to many of us, especially when we feel strongly opposed to something. Still, channeling those sentiments into an effective parody is harder than it looks.

Notes

1. Friedman, Thomas L. "A Manifesto for the Fast World." *New York Times Magazine* 28 March 1999: 40+.

2. *Psychological Operations and Psychological Warfare.* July 2002. Home page. <http://www.psywarrior.com/afghanleaf.html>.

3. "Operation Afghan Litterbug: U.S. Propaganda Leaflets in Afghanistan." Infinite Jest 2002. July 2002. <http://www.infinitejest.org:81/1/afghanistan_leaflets.html>.

4. Barton, David, and Mary Hamilton. *Local Literacies: Reading and Writing in One Commu-nity.* London: Routledge, 1998.

5. "D. C.'s Copwatch." *Harper's* December 1998: 22.

CHAPTER 3

Finding and Creating Opportunities for Public Writing

By now you've probably got a pretty good idea about what public literacy is and why people participate in it. You might even be ready to get involved in it yourself (if you haven't done so already). But participating in public literacy requires more than strong opinions and a thick magic marker. It also requires an understanding of when writing is the most effective of many possible actions and what it can realistically accomplish in a given situation.

Most of us can probably recall a time when we wished we'd said something publicly—spoken out against an injustice, corrected a misstatement in the newspaper, come to the defense of a friend—but didn't. Most of us can also probably recall a time when we *did* speak out but either wished we hadn't or later thought of a more appropriate response. Since "perfect" opportunities for public discourse may never present themselves, the purpose of this chapter is to help you to recognize *promising* opportunities for participating in national, local, everyday, and global public literacies.

Exercise

In your notebook, write about a time when you participated in public discourse (e.g., wrote a letter to the editor, attended a rally, distributed or posted flyers) or a time you thought about doing so but chose not to. Think about the reasons for your decisions and actions. What were the consequences for participating or not participating in public discourse? What, if anything, might you do differently in retrospect?

Discuss your experiences in small groups, looking for patterns. What were common motivations for participation or for lack of it? What were some common feelings afterward? What, in general, are the "best" and "worst" circumstances in which to participate in public discourse? The "best" and "worst" possible consequences?

Rhetorical Situations

As we discussed in Chapter 1, public discourse has historically been linked to rhetoric, and a central purpose of rhetoric has traditionally been to persuade an audience to support or enact some change. Most of us could easily list a dozen things we'd like to change about the world, but not all situations invite public discourse.[1]

In order to be something other than just idle performance or self-expression, public discourse must occur within a *rhetorical situation*: a set of circumstances which calls for and can be altered by oral, written, or visual communication. This response should be a natural part of the situation and may even be necessary for its completion. For example, the unofficial outcome of an election is typically marked by a concession speech on the part of the loser. This act of public literacy signals that the candidate has graciously accepted the defeat and wants her supporters to do likewise.

To say that a rhetorical situation "requires" language to complete it and that this response is a "natural" part of the situation is not to suggest that only *certain* meanings and responses are acceptable. There's nothing intrinsic about a concession speech that causes it to conclude an election; it creates that action because we agree that it does. In other words, it's simply a *convention*—a generally agreed-upon practice—that many people have come to expect and understand. Conventions aren't inflexible rules, but they can be useful as guides to what constitutes effective participation in public discourse, so it's a good idea to be aware of them.

Not all situations are rhetorical situations. In order to be "rhetorical," a situation needs to meet two criteria. First, it must be alterable: capable of being modified, corrected, improved. Second, it must be possible for this modification to be accomplished or advanced through the appropriate use of language. Imagine, for example, that you saw someone about to step in front of a car. This is a situation—a set of circumstances that requires some action or remedy. But consider which of these is the most fitting response: to yell "Hey, look out!", to go home and print up a flyer that says, "Hey, look out!", or to yank the person back onto the sidewalk?

Although this situation is alterable by several means, including appropriate use of language, it doesn't call for public literacy. But preventing *this* person from getting hit by *this* car isn't the only possible change that might be brought about by this situation. Other goals might include urging people to be more careful as they cross the street in the future, honoring citizens who do good deeds, or ensuring that busy city intersections are equipped with lighted cross-walks. All of these changes can be promoted or enacted through national, local, everyday, and global public literacies.

As this example illustrates, rhetorical situations usually invite many possible responses, and different responses can achieve different outcomes. Moreover, rhetorical situations can be created and shaped as well as discovered, depending on your goals and interests. (We will discuss this further in Chapter 4.) When you develop a habit of seeing the world rhetorically—as alterable through language—you are sure to notice many rhetorical situations.

Exercise

Skim a recent issue of your local or campus newspaper (many are available in electronic format as well as hard copy) and select one or two items that catch your interest for any reason. These could be anything—a letter in an advice column, an obituary, a concert review, a news story. Then, alone or in small groups, brainstorm a list of possible issues raised by each item you choose. For example, let's say you were reading the comics and found yourself rolling your eyes once again at how the soldiers ogle the lipstick- and miniskirt-wearing character "Miss Buxley" in *Beetle Bailey*. This could raise questions related to women in the military, whether a woman's clothes "invite" sexual harassment, or even the benefits and drawbacks of uniforms in schools and workplaces.

You may not feel particularly committed to any of these issues, but at this point your goal is simply to recognize potential rhetorical situations within the vast amount of information you process every day. The more opportunities you see to engage in public conversations, the more likely that you will find something you *are* passionate about—and the less likely you will be to roll your eyes and move on.

When Is a Rhetorical Situation Urgent?

In order to participate effectively in public discourse, it's important to recognize three components of rhetorical situations: *urgency, audience,* and *constraints.* While each of these features is integral to the rhetorical situation, urgency is initially the most important consideration and so will be the focus of the remainder of this chapter.

Urgent situations are those that require immediate action or attention in order to be improved or resolved. By weighing the *urgency* of a situation, a writer can determine whether or not it is significant enough to act upon or respond to. Public discourse is an appropriate response only when urgent situations are rhetorical—that is, capable of positive modification through discourse—and when they are in the public interest (see Chapter 1).

Some situations are urgent because they are literally matters of life or death—the person stepping in front of a car, for example. It is generally considered to be in the public interest to intervene in situations that threaten the lives, health, safety, or welfare of people (and in some cases, animals and property). Other situations, however, are urgent primarily because of a person's personal commitment to an issue or problem—perhaps for moral, ethical, or financial reasons, and perhaps because their life is directly affected by it.

Consider the example of Elsie Aldrup, a senior citizen who lives in Grand Island, Nebraska. In 1974, Mrs. Aldrup's husband, Emil, died during a stay at a local hospital.

Although he had expressed his desire not to be medicated, his requests were ignored and he was receiving 23 different drugs at the time of his death. This situation might have aroused passing sympathy or resentment in some people, but it bothered Mrs. Aldrup enough to sue for access to her husband's medical records, write letters to doctors and hospital administrators, distribute flyers around town, and erect signs in her yard, all in an effort to raise awareness about medical malpractice and patients' rights.

Or consider the example of Tarah Lyczewski from Sunnyside, Washington, who in 1999 erected an eight-foot-tall letter "A" in her front yard after finding out that her father had moved in with another woman before his divorce from Tarah's mother was final. (The display was inspired by Nathaniel Hawthorne's novel *The Scarlet Letter*.) Certainly, Tarah's conduct falls into the category of self-expression. However, it also successfully provoked vigorous local, national, and even international public debate about the issue of marital infidelity and therefore can be seen as literacy that is accessible to the public and relevant to its interests.

Sometimes even life or death situations are not considered urgent by those in a position to help. Recall the neighborhood in Washington, D.C., that was plagued by drug dealing and violence (see Chapter 2). This was an urgent situation to residents of that neighborhood, who were concerned about their safety and quality of life. However, the situation apparently wasn't urgent to local police, who ignored requests for help until publicly criticized.

The point is that situations that seem urgent to *us*—even matters of life and death—may not seem urgent to those people who could change the situations. Many of us would simply get discouraged and give up in the face of such indifference. But Elsie Aldrup, Tarah Lyczewski, and the residents of the Capitol Hill neighborhood responded by creatively transforming hopeless situations into *urgent rhetorical situations* through the strategic use of public literacy. In other words, by reimagining their problems as *alterable through public writing*, they were able to enact positive changes in their lives and communities.

Thinking Rhetorically

You might be at the point where you start seeing opportunities for public literacy everywhere. There is an infinite supply of such opportunities, and since it's impossible to respond to all of them, you should ask yourself the following questions as you consider your options for participating in public literacy:

1. Is the situation *rhetorical?*
    *   Can the situation be changed?
    *   Can I imagine ways that it might be changed through writing?
    *   Is writing an appropriate response to the situation?
    *   Is writing likely to improve the situation in any way?

If you answer "yes" to these questions, then ask yourself:

2. Is the rhetorical situation *urgent?*
    *   Does this situation affect the life, health, safety, or welfare of anyone, possibly but not necessarily including me?
        OR
    *   Does the situation matter a lot to me personally?
    *   Does the situation require an immediate response in order to be improved or completed?
    *   Is it possible that this will be the last opportunity to use writing to improve the situation?
    *   Will deferring a response make the situation worse or allow it to continue?

If you also answer "yes" to these questions, then ask yourself:

3. Is the urgent rhetorical situation *in the public interest?*
    *   Does this issue affect many people in my country, community, interpersonal network, or in some other group I care about?
    *   Are these people aware of and concerned about the issue?
    *   Would these people benefit from the change that I wish to propose?
    *   Would they support the change I wish to propose?
    *   Would they agree that some form of public literacy is a sound course of action in this situation?

If the answers to all of these questions are "yes" or "maybe," then you have probably found a promising opportunity for engaging in public literacy and should proceed with your plans. If the answer to any of these questions is "no," then you might want to reconsider whether the situation requires a written response, a public written response, or any response at all. If the answer to any of these questions is "no" but you are committed to transforming the issue into a rhetorical situation that calls for public literacy, then you might need to rethink your goals.

Exercise

Review the interests and concerns that you have listed in your writer's notebook. If you think of new ones, add them. Then, with those interests in mind, revisit some of the public spheres you identified and see if they suggest any urgent rhetorical situations; gather or record any relevant information in your notebook. The news media, Internet sites, and community bulletin boards are obvious places to start your search, but rumors, graffiti, and personal experiences can also offer promising leads. Finally, do some informal writing about how the issues on your list might be changed or improved—for example, how problems might be solved, how questions might be answered, or what kinds of small measures might set the stage for larger actions.

In small groups, share the results of your preliminary investigation, and work through the questions on the "Thinking Rhetorically" checklist above. If you think you have found a situation that invites public literacy, then you might want to start thinking about specific genres and audiences for your writing. We'll say more about this in Chapter 4.

Kimberle Brown has lived all over the United States and is studying English with the goal of teaching at the college level. Although currently unemployed, Kimberle endured years of what she calls "retail hell," during which she developed a passionate interest in women's issues and unfair labor practices. At her former job, Kimberle attempted to mobilize her coworkers around the issue of salary inequities among white and African-American women; her efforts ultimately failed, but since then Kimberle has found some satisfaction in writing letters to various companies to complain about unsatisfactory products and services.

When Kimberle reviewed her writer's notebook, she noticed that she had many questions and concerns about women's health care. Most of these concerns were inspired by her own experiences, the experiences of friends and relatives, and news reports on the spiraling costs of insurance coverage and prescription drugs. However, Kimberle was especially frustrated that the $60 health care fee she paid to her university, which was mandatory for all students and supposedly covered all Wellness Center services "free of charge." In fact, the fee does not pay for the costs of gynecological examinations, which are recommended annually for women over the age of 18 as a means of ensuring the early detection of breast and cervical cancers. After she recognized this prominent theme in her notebook, Kimberle did some informal writing and arrived at the opinion that embarassment or lack of money or insurance should not keep female students from receiving potentially life-saving medical care.

After completing the checklist above, Kimberle was convinced that women's health represents an urgent situation that the public has an interest in addressing. For one thing, the problem affects the lives and well-being of a broad cross-section of people, regardless of age, racial or ethnic background, or social class (or even, some might argue, gender). For another, health care issues are frequently the subject of national, local, global, and everyday public literacy texts (Kimberle recalled seeing flyers promoting a car wash to raise money for a local citizen who needs a kidney transplant), indicating that they are of grave concern to many citizens. Still, Kimberle couldn't figure out how she might improve women's health care through public writing: she's an English major, after all, not a doctor. Furthermore, she was certain that she would have future opportunities to respond to the problem—perhaps when she was more knowledgeable about possible solutions.

Kimberle discussed her reservations with a group of classmates, who suggested that she consider ways to *improve* the problem of insufficient health care rather than solve it—that is, to propose small steps to make the situation better, even if she couldn't figure out how to eliminate it altogether (at least not right away). They also observed that Kimberle might have a better chance of succeeding if she focused on the problem as it affected her own community. We'll examine Kimberle's response to her classmates' suggestions in Chapters 4 and 8.

Tracy ran across an article in the newspaper about how farmers in France ransacked a McDonald's to protest the restaurant's use of genetically altered beef, an issue that related to her concerns about pesticides in food. If you were Tracy's partner, how would you advise her to proceed?

Benefits, Risks, and Responsibilities

Writing for public audiences and purposes can be very satisfying, even when our efforts fall short of our goals. People who participate in public literacy regularly report feeling more knowledgeable about the world around them, more connected to their communities, and more in control of their own lives. Successful efforts can intensify one's own commitment to public issues, inspire the participation of others, and generally make the world a better place to live.

But participating in public literacy carries risks and responsibilities as well as benefits. Elsie Aldrup endured harassment, threats, and the destruction of her personal property for over 20 years as a result of her yard signs; moreover, she lost the support of many friends and neighbors, some of whom questioned her mental stability. Tarah Lyczewski became estranged from her father and was the subject of a public nuisance complaint when 208 of her neighbors filed a petition to have her display removed from her yard.

Although these situations represent unfortunate exceptions, taking responsibility for the opinions and claims you express publicly inevitably carries with it some risk. In most cases, though, the worst that happens is that people disagree with you, complain about you, or prove you wrong—sometimes just as publicly. Such consequences may make us think twice about voicing our concerns in a public sphere, but they represent a necessary risk: if people were not required to take responsibility for the claims they make publicly, then they might feel free to make untrue or libelous statements. Facing the consequences of our words, then, can encourage us to be vigilant about forming sound opinions, reporting facts accurately, being fair to other perspectives, and creating carefully edited documents.

Notes

1. Bitzer, Lloyd. "The Rhetorical Situation." *Philosophy and Rhetoric* 1 (1968): 1–14. Vatz, Richard E. "The Myth of the Rhetorical Situation." *Philosophy and Rhetoric* 6 (1973): 154–61.

CHAPTER 4

Making Decisions About Content and Form

Once you have decided that a rhetorical situation is both urgent and in the public interest, you must make a number of decisions about how to proceed with your writing. Among other things, you will need to refine your goals, select an audience, and translate your ideas into an appropriate public genre. Rhetorical situations are dynamic organisms, subject to human interpretation and manipulation as well as changing circumstances. Therefore, the decisions you make about one component of a rhetorical situation will likely affect the way you think about the whole public literacy process.

The complexity of this process can influence your efforts to participate in public literacy in positive and negative ways. On the one hand, too many decisions can be so overwhelming that they cause you to give up in frustration. But on the other hand, engaging critically with the decision-making process can assist you in imagining a range of possible responses, thus improving your chances of creating a successful public literacy document.

Choosing an Appropriate Public Genre

The content and form of public discourse are linked to genre: distinctive categories or types of writing, such as letters, poems, or reports. Documents within the same genre usually share certain conventions related to form, tone, publishing strategies, and even subject matter (see Chapters 6, 7, 8, and 9). For example, flyers usually fit on the front of one page and are generally used to announce upcoming events or offer basic information about an urgent public issue; this information often takes the form of a list rather than a narrative, and it may be centered on the sheet of paper. It would seem strange to see a flyer in the newspaper or on a website. Instead, people publish this public literacy genre by passing out copies to passers-by, putting them under windshield wipers, or posting them where they are likely to be noticed by an appropriate audience.

As a general rule, genre is not the first determination you make when you participate in public literacy. In other words, you wouldn't decide to write a press release and then search for an upcoming event to write about. You would be more likely to find yourself faced with an urgent rhetorical situation and then evaluate a variety of genre options that might allow you to respond to the situation appropriately.

Exercise

In small groups, list as many different examples of public discourse genres as you can find. This book has used flyers, public service announcements, newspapers, signs, and currency as examples of such genres, but you should be able to think of many, many others. As a class, generate a master list of public literacy genres. Continue to add to this list and use it for ongoing consultation as you begin to make decisions about how you might participate in public literacy.

Pedro Marques is a student from Herndon, Virginia, a suburb of Washington, D.C. He was born in Portugal, speaks several languages, and has traveled widely, and these experiences have influenced him to major in international business and French. Pedro is very close to his immediate and extended family and is currently assisting his father in starting his own business. His main interests are traveling, reading, and sports, which he enjoys for their own sake as well as for how they might prepare him for his career. Pedro was recently elected class president at his university and used public writing to petition for candidacy and express his platform; he has also written letters of concern to various public servants.

Pedro's list:

bumper stickers	grafitti
t-shirts	sky writing??
flyers	obituaries
memoranda	church marquee
"chalking" on campus sidewalks	report
letters to the editor	license plates
bottle caps—e.g., Nantucket Nectar	reward poster
sandwich board—"The End is Near"	buttons
grocery store bags	e-mail
action alerts on the Web	restaurant menus
"lost child" posters, milk cartons	headstones??

"Keep Valusia County Beautiful" fans passed out at baseball game

In doing this exercise, Pedro discovered that many public literacy texts, particularly everyday public literacies, are so idiosyncratic that they defy genre classification. In his writer's notebook, Pedro recorded the example of a man driving around town with a house-shaped plywood sign in the back of his truck. In red, hand-painted letters the man had written, "Don't let this happen to you. I lost $10,000 because I bought my home from Heritage Homes. They ripped me off. They're cheaters." While certainly an example of public literacy—and arguably an issue in the public interest (consumer rights)—the text was probably one of a kind.

Audience

In addition to *urgency*, rhetorical situations are composed of *audiences* and *constraints*, which we will discuss in this chapter. Considered together, these three components affect the choices you make regarding public literacy genres, public spheres, and the purposes of your writing.

An *audience* is a person or group of people to whom discourse is addressed. As with situations in general, not all audiences are rhetorical audiences.[1] In order to be "rhetorical," an audience must consist of people who are capable of two things: one, being influenced by the discourse directed toward them; and two, enacting proposed changes. In addition, audiences for public literacy must have access to the document you prepare (e.g., must be able to read the language in which it is written).

Unless it is composed of people who are utterly indifferent to the issue, have profound moral or ethical objections to the actions you propose, or are mentally disabled, an audience is generally receptive to suggestions for improving a situation. However, even those people who have been persuaded by your discourse might not be able—or willing—to take the actions you propose. For instance, inmates residing in federal penitentiaries might agree that one candidate would make the best president, but they are not allowed to vote. Other voters might agree that the candidate is the most qualified but be unconvinced that their vote will make any difference in the outcome of the election.

Clearly, audiences don't have to be convicted felons to be incapable of carrying out desired changes. Their capacity might also be affected by lack of transportation, limited financial resources, insufficient time, physical disability, moral or ethical objections, fear, apathy, age, different priorities, and a whole host of personal distractions. These factors need not disqualify audiences from hearing your message, but they might cause you to rethink your rhetorical goals.

In Chapter 2 we examined the ways in which different countries use money as a public forum through which they can assert a national identity and advance national interests. Money also illustrates how access to public discourse can be affected by issues other than language. Recently, the American Council of the Blind sued the United States federal government seeking changes in the design of banknotes; specifically, they requested that they be printed in Braille and that the height and length of bills be varied according to denomination so that they could be more easily distinguished by people with visual impairments. The organization sued under a provision in the Rehabilitation Act of 1973 which states that individuals with disabilities may not be excluded from or denied the benefits of participation in any program or activity conducted by the U.S. government—including the printing and circulation of currency and the ability to freely make purchases.

Fortunately, most decisions about content and form don't require a federal lawsuit, even if they deal with national issues. The point, though, is that the content and form of your writing are intimately influenced by who your audience is.[2] For example, if the goal of your writing were to encourage the President of the United States to allocate more money for student loans, you probably wouldn't put up flyers around campus (unless, of course, the President was visiting your campus). However, if your goal was to encourage *students* to put pressure on the President to do this, campus might be an appropriate public sphere and flyers an appropriate genre. Since the purpose of public literacy is to set in motion actions in the public interest—or at least create in your audience a willingness to act at the appropriate time (e.g., vote in an election)—you need to be aware of what your audience regards as logical, true, fair, correct, and compelling.

But understanding your audience is often as challenging as it is necessary, for like rhetorical situations—and, indeed, like public spheres—audiences are not fixed, stable entities. Even if it is friendly and familiar (perhaps made up of people like you), an audience is likely to be disorganized and multiform; thus it can't simply be "addressed" as if its members were sitting in a room together, politely waiting for you to tell them what to do (which hardly ever happens). Sometimes it is necessary to "invoke" an audience instead of addressing it—that is, create or summon the "ideal" audience.[3] As the Capitol Hill flyer in Chapter 2 illustrates, language can be a powerful means to do this: instead of saying "Attention, Police: Please Help Us!" (a strategy that had been ineffective), the flyer subtly *invokes* an audience of caring law enforcement officers who would assist the residents with their problem.

Constraints

Writers must also consider how their public literacy efforts might be undermined or "constrained." *Constraints* describe any factors that complicate the writing of your document or an audience's reaction to it. They range from the very abstract (e.g., beliefs, values, motivations) to the very concrete (e.g., time, weather, money), from the minor (e.g., the copy shop is closed) to the virtually insurmountable (e.g., you don't speak the audience's language).

Although some mitigating circumstances can't be prevented, writers must try to anticipate as many constraints as possible so that they can revise their plans and goals accordingly. If you find yourself making excuses for why you can't engage in public literacy, then the rhetorical situation you've identified probably isn't as urgent or as important to you as you originally thought.

Even circumstances that seem to lie outside the rhetorical situation can constrain public literacy efforts. Let's say, for example, that two days before student government elections, one candidate's staff posts flyers that feature a police mug shot of her opponent and the following message: "Is this the man you want handling your budget?" Maybe the accused candidate considers a response urgently important but has no money to create his own flyers or buy a radio spot. Or maybe he has three papers due that week, is sick, or thinks that his opponent's flyers won't really be that damaging. Thus external events and human judgments are introduced into the rhetorical situation, constraining possible responses.

Thinking Rhetorically

At this point, you have probably identified several urgent rhetorical situations that might be answered through public literacy. As you consider your options, generate a list of audiences that might find each rhetorical situation urgent (or that might be *persuaded* to find it urgent). Then for each audience, ask yourself the following questions:

1. Is the *audience* rhetorical?
    *   Are its members capable of being influenced by my writing?
    *   Are they capable of carrying out any actions I wish to propose?
    *   Can this audience be addressed or invoked through writing?
    *   Are its members likely to notice my document?
    *   Is my message likely to meet with their support?

If you answer "yes" to these questions, then make a list of public literacy genres that might be appropriate to your rhetorical situation (you should have a list in your writer's notebook). For each genre, ask yourself the following questions:

2. Is this *genre* suitable for this rhetorical situation?
    *   Is it appropriate to my message?
    *   Does my intended audience have access to it?
    *   Is my audience likely to find it interesting and worthy of their attention?

If you also answer "yes" to these questions, then ask yourself:

3. Are there any *constraints* I can anticipate?
    *   Do I have the time, commitment, and resources to create an appropriate public literacy document?

- Do I have the skills necessary to create an appropriate document? If not, do I know anyone who has these skills, or can I obtain the skills in a timely fashion?

- Do I have the knowledge and information about this *issue* to create an appropriate document? If not, am I willing and able to do the necessary research?

- Do I have the knowledge and information about this *genre* to create an appropriate document? If not, am I willing and able to do the necessary research?

- Do I have the knowledge and information about this *audience* to create an appropriate document? If not, am I willing and able to do the necessary research?

- Am I willing to accept the risks and consequences of publishing my literacy document?

If the answers to all of these questions are "yes" or "maybe," then you have probably identified an audience and genre appropriate to your rhetorical situation, with few or minor constraints.

If the answer to any of these questions is "no," then you should work through the checklist again with different audiences, different genres, different goals—or different combinations of all of these—in mind. If you can't find a combination that seems to work, then you might want to reconsider whether to respond to this rhetorical situation, however urgent it might be. If the answer to any of these questions is "no" but you are committed to transforming the issue into a rhetorical situation that calls for public literacy, then you might need to rethink your goals or enlist a partner to assist you in your efforts.

Answering "no" to any of the items related to constraints does not necessarily mean that you should give up your plans to participate in public literacy. It simply means that you will face some challenges. If you are very interested in or committed to the issue, however, you can probably meet these challenges successfully. Carolyn McCarthy knew nothing about guns or politics until her husband was killed and her son seriously injured during a mass shooting on the Long Island Railroad in 1993. But she took the time and energy to find out, and now she's a member of the United States House of Representatives, using national public literacies to enact changes in laws regulating the ownership of assault weapons.

Exercise

Alone or in small groups, go back to the urgent rhetorical situation(s) you identified in Chapter 3. Then, work through the questions on the "Thinking Rhetorically" checklist above. By the end of this exercise, you should have at least one concrete plan for creating a public literacy document. Don't hesitate to think about rhetorical situations from multiple perspectives—that is, in ways that fit *your* motivations, commitments, skills, and beliefs. Remember, too, that plans are only "drafts" and can be revised as circumstances dictate.

Challenge yourself to identify several rhetorical situations every week. The more options you have, the more likely you are to find a situation that you want to respond to.

Let's return now to the rhetorical situation outlined by Kimberle in Chapter 3. Concerned about the inadequacy of women's health care and the prohibitive costs of obtaining it, Kimberle wanted to make health care more accessible to women in her community. She was initially skeptical about how writing might help to accomplish this ambitious goal, so in response to her peers' advice, she set a more modest objective of asking university officials to commit to covering the costs of gynecological exams for uninsured female students on her campus. Kimberle then made a list of local public spheres that might assist her in promoting her cause; these included the campus Women's Resource Center and Wellness Center; advocacy organizations for cancer research and treatment; the campus newspaper and radio stations; and a variety of websites related to women's issues, health care, and cancer.

In response to the first two questions on the checklist, Kimberle settled on the idea of writing to the Chancellor of her university, asking him to allocate money in the university budget for free gynecological exams. Upon further reflection, however, she recognized several constraints to her plan—among them, that the Chancellor would not be likely to take seriously a request for money submitted by an individual student, however persuasive her argument. In short, Kimberle needed to bolster her credibility by affiliating with an established advocacy group; unfortunately, she didn't know of any. This realization caused Kimberle to reconsider her preliminary decisions regarding goals, audience, and genre.

Discouraged, Kimberle turned once again to her group for assistance. This time they urged her to talk to a classmate, Summer Stanger, an education major from Fayetteville, North Carolina. In their first conversation, Kimberle learned that Summer had recently had a frustrating experience at the Wellness Center and was interested in collaborating on a project that might improve services there. Although Summer had no prior experience participating in public discourse, she had an abiding interest in women's health, population growth, and the environment. She also loves Irish literature and recently returned from a study abroad trip to Ireland. Although she grew up in a small community, Summer enjoys big cities and would like to return to Europe one day, possibly to teach.

Summer and Kimberle discussed their shared concerns, and since neither of them were aware of any local organizations that advocated on behalf of female students' health care needs, they took the bold step of establishing one (see "Case in Point" below). In an effort to evoke the life-threatening nature of cervical cancer, they settled on the name "FACT of Life: Females Against

Cost of Treatment of Life." And after working through the checklist a few more times, Kimberle and Summer eventually decided to write a grant proposal to establish a fund that would cover the costs of well woman care for uninsured students.

At first glance, Kimberle and Summer's plans may seem several steps removed from the problem of inadequate health care for women—and indeed, Kimberle herself might initially have envisioned a more "glamorous" response to the problem, such as testifying before Congress or spearheading a national student movement for more affordable wellness services. But her revised goals are more achievable, and when met, they can encourage more ambitious efforts on the part of Kimberle, Summer, and others. It's worth remembering that public literacy doesn't have to garner a lot of attention or accolades to be effective. It only has to set realistic goals and reach the audience for whom it is intended.

Four Public Literacy Genres in Action

With so many possible combinations of urgency, audience, constraints, genres, and public spheres, it's not hard to understand why many writers abandon their public literacy goals in frustration. So let's look at an extended example of how the process of thinking rhetorically invites national, local, everyday, and global public literacies.

James Cooper and Chandler Snyder are avid bicyclists, but they were frustrated by the lack of safe bike lanes and convenient mass transit options in the city where they attend college and also by the apparent lack of student interest in a shuttle bus initiative designed to reduce the number of cars on campus. James and Chandler quickly concluded that these are indeed urgent rhetorical situations in the interest of their local public. They had a general sense of their goals—to improve alternative transportation options in the city and on campus—and brainstormed several more specific solutions before deciding to proceed:

> participate in Critical Mass rides
>
> ask City Council (Department of Transportation?) to build bike lanes
>
> start a Yellow Bike program
>
> see if there are any tax breaks for cities that invest in alternative transportation infrastructure
>
> write letters to editors of school and local paper encouraging them to use the shuttle
>
> distribute maps of existing bike routes in city (also shuttle schedules?)
>
> public service announcements—raise awareness about biking or campus shuttle?

work for candidates who support the building of bike lanes

e-mail campaign?

James and Chandler realized that several of their ideas represented *physical* rather than *rhetorical* actions. In particular, they were concerned that Critical Mass rides (where large groups of bicyclists clog streets during rush hours to protest dependency on cars) might be construed as annoying expressions of self interest rather than persuasive calls for action. They thought they might be able to promote such actions through writing, but agreed that these solutions were less likely to influence non-cyclists.

After working through the "Thinking Rhetorically" checklists, James and Chandler decided that they wanted to start a Yellow Bike program, in which bicycles are painted yellow and left around a city or campus, unlocked, for common use. They anticipated several constraints, including lack of money and bikes, but mapped out a four-step process that they hoped would allow them to establish the program gradually: first, collect as many donated bikes as possible; second, obtain funding to refurbish and paint the bikes and promote the program; third, organize a group of people to maintain the bikes and monitor the success of the program; and finally, obtain funding to expand the program to the local community.

1. Everyday Public Literacies

In order to solicit donations for the Yellow Bike program and encourage others to join their efforts, Chandler and James, with the help of supportive friends, created and posted flyers at local bike stores and second-hand stores and on community bulletin boards; using a campus-wide e-mail distribution list, they sent messages to all faculty and staff; on weekends, they combed rummage sales and salvage yards. Their efforts yielded them 38 donated bikes—some nearly new, others in various states of disrepair.

Chandler, James, and their friends represent an informal network of people engaged in purposeful public literacy work (as well as physical effort). Although their goals are designed to serve a broader public interest—that is, to benefit people other than themselves, including people they don't know—no one is monitoring or controlling their efforts. Significantly, the public spheres where they chose to publicize their project required little or no financial investment on their part and no application or approval processes.

2. Local Public Literacies

Because they believed their project would improve the lives of the entire campus community, Chandler and James decided to ask their Student Government Association for money to paint and refurbish the bikes they had collected. They picked up a copy of the SGA "Special Activity Fund Request Form and Guidelines" (see Chapter 8), at which point they encountered their first major obstacle: the application required Chandler and James to list the name of their campus organization and the number of members, but they hadn't yet formed an organization.

So Chandler and James revised their original plan, arranging a meeting for everyone who had donated bikes or expressed interest in their project. At this meeting, the group decided to call themselves "SCAT: Students and Community for Alternative Transportation"—and drafted a mission statement that articulated its goals and ideals. Chandler and James then filled out the Special Activity Fund application on behalf of SCAT, submitted the necessary copies, and presented their proposal the SGA Appropriations Committee, which awarded the group $500.

Just because Chandler and James established a formal organization doesn't mean that SCAT can no longer participate in everyday public literacies. Indeed, grassroots organizing and everyday literacies might be the most effective means to accomplish their goals. However, most everyday publics exist within local contexts—institutions, traditions, even prejudices specific to a geographical place—that both enable and constrain public literacy efforts. Engaging in local public literacies often obligates writers to accept institutional procedures and writing conventions.

3. National Public Literacies

James and Chandler were initially satisfied with obtaining nominal funding to launch the Yellow Bike program and SCAT on campus. With an eye toward expanding the program, however, they applied for nonprofit or "501(c)(3)" status, which would, among other things, exempt SCAT's tiny budget from federal taxation and entitle the group to reduced postal rates. The incorporation process was long and confusing and involved filling out several federal forms, revising SCAT's mission statement, and establishing bylaws and a board of directors.

National public literacies make it legal for James and Chandler to undertake every idea on their original list, if they so choose. The First Amendment, for example, guarantees their write to participate in peaceful Critical Mass rides or distribute documents promoting their ideas.

But some national documents, such as those that James filled out to establish SCAT as a nonprofit corporation, do more than make public literacy possible: they actually encourage it by providing access to a national public sphere or by offering resources, support, and legal protection to members of a national public. Some of these literacies—such as the IRS publication "Application for Recognition of Exemption," which details eligibility requirements and procedures for applying for federal tax exempt status—are sponsored by the federal government, but many are made available by groups or organizations working in the national public interest.

4. Global Public Literacies

Interest in alternative modes of transportation is not limited to Chandler and James's campus or even to the United States. Cars and gasoline are prohibitively expensive in many parts of the world and most industrialized nations are trying to reduce their reliance on automobiles because of concerns about pollution, urban sprawl, road rage, and even obesity. Aware of this international movement, Chandler and James began to investigate ways in which their Yellow Bike program might participate in ongoing global conversations about these pressing issues.

They focused their attention on an international event similar to Critical Mass: the Day Without Cars in Bogotà, Columbia, which has allowed only cars and buses within city limits on one day a year since 1999 (violators face $25 fines). Although neither Chandler nor James had the financial means to fly to Bogotà to participate in the Day Without Cars, they did have public literacy at their disposal. So on February 7 they took three actions: first, they persuaded the foreign languages offices at their university to use their international cable service to televise Columbian news coverage of the event; second, they set up an information booth at the student union to inform passers-by about alternative transportation; and finally, they staged a "sympathetic" Critical Mass ride to express solidarity with the walkers, skaters, and cyclists elsewhere in the world—an event which garnered media coverage of its own.

Establishing the Yellow Bike program on campus was not as easy as it might sound here; it took several months, and James and Chandler encountered many obstacles along the way. Their efforts were further constrained by the fact that they are both serious students with a variety of other interests and commitments. At the same time, their actions provide a good example of how public literacy can intervene in a specific problem on many levels.

Exercise

Alone or in small groups, go to the website *www.ask.com* (or use another search engine of your choice) to find information about how to apply for or 501(c)(3) status. Choose a few websites from the search results and look through them. In what ways do federal procedures for obtaining nonprofit status facilitate or constrain participation in national public literacies? In your opinion, are the requirements reasonable for an "average person" who wants to establish a nonprofit organization? Do you learn anything new about public literacy from your inquiry into 501(c)(3)s?

As you decipher these federal guidelines, reflect on the circumstances under which you might want to expand your public literacy efforts into national or global arenas and those under which it would be preferable to focus on everyday or local public spheres.

Notes

1. Bitzer, Lloyd F. "The Rhetorical Situation." *Philosophy and Rhetoric* 1 (1968): 1–14.

2. Fisher, Walter R. *Human Communication as Narration.* Columbia: U of South Carolina P, 1987. Perelman, Chaim, and L. Olbrechts-Tyteca. *The New Rhetoric: A Treatise on Argumentation.* Notre Dame, IN: U of Notre Dame P, 1969.

3. Ede, Lisa, and Andrea Lunsford. "Audience Addressed/Audience Invoked: The Role of Audience in Composition Theory and Pedagogy." *College Composition and Communication* 35 (1984): 155–71.

CHAPTER 5

Research in the Public Interest

There may be times when you have to do additional research in order to respond to a rhetorical situation effectively. The nature of that research will depend upon the rhetorical situation. For example, if an urgent rhetorical situation requires an immediate response, you may not have time to pore over archival documents or interview several people; this may in turn constrain your choice of audience and genre. In other situations, though, lack of knowledge or information can actually inspire your participation in public literacy.

National public literacy documents apply equally to all members of that public and are generally accessible to all *readers*; however, they are usually *written* by a small minority of people within that diverse public sphere. Conversely, everyday public literacy documents are accessible to all readers and writers within a social or political network but circulate with little oversight and so have few hard and fast "rules"; the same is true of many global public literacy documents. For these reasons, this chapter will focus on research in the local public sphere, including how to use local sources, how to gain "insider knowledge" about a community, and how to translate academic knowledge into local contexts.

Local Knowledge

Sometimes the concept of a public sphere can seem so abstract and complex as to be incomprehensible—and hence inaccessible. In such circumstances, it can be useful to turn our attention to *local knowledge*: what "everybody knows" about a community, like what the "good schools" and "bad neighborhoods" are, where to find the freshest produce or the best live music. Like everyday public literacies, local knowledge is informal and largely uncontrolled by official institutions. It describes what is recognized as true, correct, and worthwhile by a community, and the ways in which those beliefs are influenced by histories, memories, traditions, and language within a specific geographical setting.[1] Paying attention to local knowledge can enrich our understanding of cultural practices such as public literacy and increase our opportunities to participate in them effectively.

Even in the smallest, most apparently homogeneous communities, local knowledges are negotiated by various public and private actions, special interest groups, and texts. The more diverse a community, the more likely that its history, values, and beliefs will be contested. Many residents might agree on the "bad neighborhoods," for example, but have very different perspectives on *why* a neighborhood is considered "bad," how it came to be "bad" in the first place, and who's responsible for improving it. These perspectives are not always debated openly or amicably; some interests may be represented more conspicuously or more favorably in public discourse, and others may not be represented at all. In fact, local knowledge is often unspoken—something people "just know" but don't talk about or write down.

At the same time, much local knowledge is mediated by written language, whether through national or local literacies (e.g., laws), everyday or global literacies, or professional literacies like advertising and journalism. Members of a local public who can read and write regularly use language to engage with and make sense of the world—often so unconsciously that we take it for granted. We read newspapers and write letters to editors, we file insurance claims and appeal hospital charges, we vote and work to elect candidates whose platforms we support. Such actions allow us not just to acquire local knowledge but to actively create it. In doing so we become shareholders in local knowledge, using literacy to empower ourselves and others.

Local knowledge does have its limitations. Because it is situated in a specific time and place, it may offer few insights into the culture practices of other communities, even those that appear to be similar. Moreover, because it evolves over time, it's virtually impossible to grasp local knowledge fully, especially if you're a new resident. Still, local knowledge is part of the full matrix of intellectual life within a community, and its significance can't be disregarded.

Of course, there's no "Book of Local Knowledge" to demystify all this. But research can offer insight into local knowledge as well as mobilize it in the public interest.

Four Approaches to Local Research

1. Consulting Local Sources

Every day we encounter texts, sites, services, and artifacts so ordinary and familiar that we might underestimate them as sources of information. These local sources include:

Local newspapers	Newscasts	Bills
Telephone books and directories	Library collections	Agency brochures
Festivals and other events	Laws and ordinances	Landmarks
Maps and guidebooks	Local museum exhibits	Local fact books
Municipal hearings	Citations and summons	Billboards

While almost all communities make some of these sources available to the local public—often at no cost—the information contained within them is specific to each setting and contributes to a body of local knowledge that is virtually unique.

Local sources can reveal much about the character of a place, in ways that range from the whimsical to the weighty to the downright baffling. For example, signs welcoming visitors to Sumner, Washington, proclaim it to be the "Rhubarb Pie Capital of the USA," while signs at the outskirts of Clarkson Valley, Missouri, proudly announce, "Less government is good government." Such information is more than merely interesting: it also offers insight into what these communities value, how they define themselves, and what they consider to be in the public interest.

The depth, timeliness, and accuracy of local source materials varies widely. Some, like daily newspapers, are able to provide up-to-date and detailed analysis of current events, while others, such as maps, generally offer little or no interpretation and may become out-dated within months.

Even relatively superficial texts can be rich sources of local information. Consider telephone books: simply looking through the government "blue pages" can not only expand your understanding of government duties but also introduce you to bureaucratic structures. Phone books can guide you to government offices and nonprofit or philanthropic organizations, many of which provide literature to community residents at no charge. This information can in turn assist you in researching issues in the public interest and making informed choices about how to participate in public literacy.

Many local sources represent official perspectives designed to provide members of a local public (including tourists or other non-residents) with information and give them a sense of shared identity. This is not to say, however, that local sources offer a single version of local knowledge that everyone accepts as true. In fact, they may tell conflicting stories, thus revealing tensions in local knowledge and leaving you with more questions than answers about a community. Local knowledge is defined as much by what local sources exclude as by what they include, which is why it's important to read them critically.

Sometimes local knowledge can be found in national sources. If you want to find demographic information about a community (e.g., statistics related to race, age, income, education, pet ownership, housing costs, bankruptcies filed), the following sources—all available at most libraries as well as on the Internet, and all updated regularly—are good places to start[2]:

Print Sources:

Statistical Abstract of the United States and *American FactFinder*: wide range of economic, social, and political statistics, gleaned mostly from government sources and published by the U.S. Bureau of the Census

http://www.census.gov/stat_abstract/
http://www.census.gov/main/www/subjects.html
http://factfinder.census.gov/servlet/BasicFactsServlet

Information Please, Almanac, Atlas and Yearbook: information on popular culture in addition to statistics and links to other reference sites

http://www.infoplease.com

Facts on File: A Weekly World News Digest: "history as it happens"; current events news
distilled from various media sources; web version updated weekly

http://www.facts.com

Almanac of American Politics: information about contemporary federal and state politics
and politicians

http://nationaljournal.qpass.com/members/almanac/

If you're not sure where to turn, you might begin by taking a look at the site
http://www.refdesk.com, which bills itself as "the single best source for facts on the
Net." Although heavy on factoids and trivia, the site also includes links to current
news and weather sources, search engines, dictionaries, encyclopedias, maps, geneal-
ogy records, software, phone books, writing handbooks, and more.

Exercise

Do a *content analysis* of a local newspaper: a detailed list of topics, issues,
themes, and perspectives represented within it. To do this, skim every issue
for at least a month, focusing on front page headlines; any section whose focus is local, regional, or "neighborhood" news; and the opinion pages, including letters to the editor. In your writer's notebook, make a list of recurring themes, names of people who are mentioned repeatedly, ongoing local
debates, and so on, recording the number of references. As you do your content analysis, take note of other newspaper features that might reflect local
values—for example, special interest pages or columns, comic strips, and the
proportion of locally written versus syndicated material.

Now do a content analysis of at least one other kind of local source—the
phone book, for example, or a visitors' guide. If your community publishes
more than one newspaper—an "alternative" weekly, for example—you may
also choose to analyze this source, comparing and contrasting it to a more
"mainstream" newspaper.

Then, in small groups, consolidate your content analyses and see if you can
come up with a composite description of your local community. In general,
what are the people like? What do they seem to care about, value, enjoy?

What bothers them? What unites and divides them? How do they characterize themselves? What groups are prominantly represented in local public discourse? What groups are underrepresented or invisible? What issues or perspectives get talked about a lot, not much, or not at all? What tensions in local knowledge can you observe? What questions emerge from these tensions or contradictions?

Pedro initially found this exercise difficult because he lives in the Washington, D.C., area, where the local culture is often indistinguishable from the national culture of government, the museums of the Smithsonian Institution, and a host of national landmarks. Even the "local newspaper"—the *Washington Post*—enjoys a national circulation. In response to this dilemma, Pedro and his classmates decided to search for less prominent local sources, such as suburban newspapers and phone books, that serve more distinct local publics.

If you live in a very large, cosmopolitan, or nationally prominent city like Pedro, it may be more fruitful for you to think of it as composed of many local publics. If this proves too difficult, you might want to use local sources to try to define a national public: by reading locally published newspapers with national circulations, visiting local museums of national culture, and so on, what conclusions can you draw about what this country values? What stories does our country like to tell about itself? What issues and perspectives does it consider important or marginal? What gaps, tensions, or conflicts do national sources reveal?

Tracy's response to the exercises appears later in this chapter.

2. Gaining "Insider Knowledge"

In the book *Midnight in the Garden of Good and Evil*, writer John Berendt runs across a reference to "Sadie Jefferson" in a 1914 Savannah newspaper and later looks in the city directory to find out who this woman was. When he finds no record of her, a librarian takes one look at his newspaper clipping and immediately informs him that he has consulted the wrong part of the directory. Noting that the courtesy title "Miss" or "Mrs." had been omitted from the reference, the librarian concluded that Sadie Jefferson was African American and thus would be listed in the "Colored" section of the city directory.[3]

Berendt wasn't even aware that there *was* a "Colored" section of the directory. But the bigger lesson to be learned from this experience is that local knowledge is more than the sum of its parts—more, in other words, than a list of phone numbers, names, dates, and historical sites. Making sense of these bits and pieces of information often requires more than the official interpretations provided by local public literacy sources. It can require the "insider knowledge" of people who have lived in a community for a long time—a deeply contextualized understanding of what characterizes it as a place. Usually we develop this kind of knowledge over time, as we live in a community and learn its conventions and idiosyncracies. There are ways to expedite this process, however, and one of these is to interview longtime residents.[4]

Choosing an Informant

The purpose of this type of interview is to gain insights that aren't available elsewhere, particularly those that community "outsiders" do not yet have the resources to understand. Longtime residents of a community make ideal informants, particularly if they can offer perspectives that are not well represented in local public documents. You may already know some people who would be good sources of insider knowledge. If you don't, neighbors, friends, professors, and family members may be able to suggest good informants, as can the Advancement Office or Alumni Association at your college.

Even if you already possess an insider's understanding of your community's local knowledge, you can still learn from an interview. Talking to a longtime resident who has experienced the community differently than you have—because of differences in age, physical ability, race, or socioeconomic status, for example—will surely yield fresh insights into local knowledge.

The most important criteria when choosing informants is that they have an interest in your subject and a willingness to talk to you. Another important consideration, however, is maturity. A teenager who has lived in the same community his whole life will certainly possess significant insider knowledge. An older person, however, might be more experienced at reflecting on his knowledge and connecting it to larger networks of information and experience. (This varies from informant to informant, of course.)

Asking Good Questions

It's vital that you prepare your questions and review them carefully in advance so that you can devote your full attention to your informant during the interview. Crafting good questions can be difficult, but a good way to get started is to make a list of reasons why you are interested in talking to your informant and then use this list to develop your initial questions. For example, if you chose your informant because she was active in local government for many years, you might ask her how she became involved in politics. These kinds of questions can introduce you to interesting personal and local histories as well as set the tone of your interview. They can also steer your informant away from answers that are superficial or uncritical or that simply parrot the Chamber of Commerce version of local knowledge.

Since the goal of your interview is to gain insider knowledge, you should ask questions that invite your informant to reflect on and interpret information. Questions that begin with "Why" or "How" can facilitate this process, while questions that elicit simple "yes" or "no" answers do not. If you don't understand an answer or want to know more, ask follow-up questions: "Why is that?" "Can you explain what you mean?" "I'd like to go back to something you said earlier. . . ." Needless to say, you should never interrupt or argue with an informant; wait for an appropriate time to ask follow-up questions, and offer your own opinions only when your informant solicits them.

During the interview, your most important role is to listen carefully to what your informant is saying. Simply put: your informant should be doing most of the talking. Don't worry if they don't respond right away. If you ask good questions, they might need some time to think about their answers.

Interview Etiquette

Not all interviews will go smoothly: some informants may be shy, reserved, or self-conscious; you might even be nervous yourself. Still, you can make the most of an interview by coming prepared, listening attentively, and being flexible if the interview takes an unexpected turn. If possible, ask a partner to review your questions and practice the interview with you ahead of time so that you are comfortable listening and taking notes at the same time. It can also be helpful to give your informant a copy of the questions before the interview so that they will have time to think through their answers; this can help you to avoid uncomfortable silences or unfocused answers during the interview.

Although people who grant you interviews are important local sources, you can't treat them as you might the local library or history museum. In other words, you can't just show up at their door, ask them some questions off the top of your head, and leave. Always schedule the interview as far in advance as possible and confirm your appointment a day or two ahead of time. Be sure to arrive on time and dress conservatively; come prepared with a list of questions, your writer's notebook, writing utensils, and, if practicable, a tape recorder. After the interview, write or call your informant to thank them for sharing their time and knowledge with you, and offer to give them a copy of any writing that makes use of their contribution.

Exercise

Go back to the content analyses of local sources that you recorded in your writer's notebook and identify information that you found confusing or contradictory. Then ask around for names of community insiders who could help you to interpret this information (these may include people mentioned in related articles); record these names in your writer's notebook. Arrange to interview at least one of these people with the purpose of enhancing your own local knowledge. You may wish to focus your interview on collecting stories about what your community used to be like or how it has changed over the years. Or you may wish to take advantage of this opportunity to gain insights into the questions you raised in your content analyses.

Prepare a draft of your interview questions in advance, and ask a partner to read them with an eye toward revision.

3. Going On-Line

Because the Internet has both expanded the range of available public spheres and facilitated our access to information related to other public spheres (e.g., government offices and nonprofit agencies), on-line research has become an important source of local knowledge. Most cities—as well as counties, states, and other regional consortia—now sponsor websites related to government services and operations, local commissions and boards, NGOs (non-governmental organizations, usually nonprofits), business, real estate, and recreation and tourism.

It isn't difficult to find these pages. One way is to use directories made available through popular search engines, which may include "government" as a category; simply type in the name of the city, county, or other entity and conduct your search. Another, probably more direct, route is through a portal or gateway website like one of the following:

> *State and Local Government on the Net*
>> http://www.statelocalgov.net

> *GovSpot.com*: also includes federal government sites at the FirstGov link
>> http://www.govspot.com

> *Library of Congress*
>> http://lcweb.loc.gov/global/state/stategov.html

> *National Association of Chief Information Officers*: includes information on nonprofit organizations as well as government entities
>> http://www.nascio.org/statesearch

The advantage of these kinds of sites is that they offer reasonably comprehensive and current information about government services, regulations, and personnel. The main disadvantage, however, is that they typically exclude sites that might otherwise provide the intangible insights that are the heart of local knowledge: personal pages, neighborhood pages, political advocacy and campaign pages, information related to NGOs that meet gaps in governmental services (e.g., literacy councils, traveler assistance programs), newspapers, and more.

You may be able to locate relevant websites by doing a keyword or subject search, which will link you to sites sponsored by the local Chamber of Commerce or United Way, as well as independent sites not affiliated with these groups. Telephone directories for most cities are available on-line through various "white pages" and "yellow pages" links. Most search engines also list personal pages under the "people" category and feature "News" links that can take you to thousands of international, national, local, and even campus newspapers (Google lists over 600 student newspapers alone). Again, the advantage of this kind of search is that you open yourself to surprises; the disadvantage is that you may have to sift through a lot of chaff to find the wheat.

Having information about local government, business services, and nonprofit agencies at your fingertips can save a lot of time and aggravation, especially on weekends or during non-business hours. Despite the convenience, however, it's unwise to depend too heavily on electronic sources—and not just because inopportune power outages, viruses, and technical glitches pose constant threats. For there are significant differences between *information* and *knowledge*, even though the two are often equated.

The fact of the matter is that we acquire much of our local knowledge through a kind of osmosis, without conscious awareness of what we know until we need to activate that knowledge. And while the Internet and electronic databases give us access to lots of information, they don't necessarily give us the tools to understand it. Computers, moreover, only allow us to take in one screen at a time; they are two-dimensional, hence inhospitable to peripheral vision and decidedly lacking in overheard snatches of conversation and scraps of paper clinging to a community kiosk. Of course, it's certainly possible to "browse" the Internet in the hopes of stumbling across something interesting, but this can be time-consuming, frustrating, haphazard, and full of distractions.

In short, electronic methods of research work best when you already know what you're looking for. Which is why in the end, nothing can beat the basics: talking to people, following local news and politics from a variety of perspectives, and paying attention to what's going on around you. If you are committed to doing significant portions of your research on-line, the DataCenter website (*http://www.datacenter.org/research*) offers excellent guidance on everything from planning a research strategy to evaluating on-line sources to choosing a search engine.

Exercise

Alone or in small groups, generate a list of questions you have about life in your city or the people who live there—whom to contact about a problem, how to get something done, that sort of thing.

Pedro and a group of his classmates came up with the following list:

Can I pay a parking ticket on-line?

What are the details of the new noise ordinance? Why does the Firebelly Lounge keep getting cited for it?

Are there any groups that support people with breast cancer?

Are there any gay advocacy groups? When do they meet and what do they do?

Where can I find organic produce?

Who do I complain to about the potholes on my street?

My friend's landlord still hasn't returned his security deposit. What rights
does he have? Is there a lawyer who will help him for free?

Is skateboarding illegal downtown?

Are there any residents who were active in the USO during World War II?

What internships are available in the Parks and Recreation office?

What kinds of fertilizers or pesticides are used on city parks?

Have there been any brutality charges filed against local police officers?

After you have generated a good list, use any of the on-line search strategies
described above (or others you might know of) to see if you can find answers
to your questions. As you do your research, enhance your local knowledge by
following any links that capture your interest. What obstacles, if any, did you
encounter in your search? How do the websites you explore make it easy or
difficult to locate the information you need? Are there some kinds of information that different sites seem to emphasize or exclude?

In their research, Pedro and his group became fascinated with the arcane and
seemingly arbitrary guidelines for enforcing city noise ordinances. Further research revealed that these ordinances had been instituted only within the last
year and remained the subject of lively debate among downtown residents,
business owners, and patrons. Concerned that their favorite night spot, the
Firebelly Lounge, had been unfairly singled out for violating these new ordinances, Pedro and several of his friends decided to take action. Their efforts
are detailed in Chapter 9.

4. Translating Academic Research

Local knowledge can be more meaningful within the context of the larger world of
people, events, and ideas that you are learning about in school—and vice versa. There
will probably be many instances where you feel that a local public would benefit from
academic knowledge, perhaps because it can shed light on or even provide solutions to
local problems in the public interest. Sharing academic research can be a responsible
way to contribute to local knowledge, but it can also be a bit tricky.

Whenever you use research to enhance the persuasiveness of your writing, it is absolutely vital that you consult the kinds of sources that will be valued by your audience and use these sources according to conventions your audience expects and un-
derstands. In an academic setting, your audience will primarily consist of college
professors, most of whom value some form of academic research—that is, the kind
found in professional books and journals and which includes theoretical discussions, experimental data, and interpretations offered by other experts with academic
credentials. Academic research writing conventions vary from discipline to discipline; much of the writing and research you will be asked to do in college is de-

signed to introduce you to these conventions so that you will be able to use them skillfully in college and your career.

When writing public literacy documents, however, you almost never rely on the disciplinary jargon and documentation conventions you practice in college. These features of academic writing represent a kind of shorthand: not only do people who write in academic settings understand what these features signify, but they also recognize their users as academic insiders—people who have subject matter knowledge and have been socialized into the conventions of their discipline. People who read and write outside of an academic context may find such conventions confusing, unnecessary, or even pretentious.

Likewise, a local public audience may prefer some styles or genres over others—for example, local histories presented through museum exhibits rather than books written by professors using obscure theories and documents, or informational brochures rather than scientific studies. The problem is not simply that a public audience might find these sources difficult to understand; it's that they might feel that academic knowledge obscures rather than illuminates local issues. It is the responsibility of the writer to anticipate these possible constraints before creating a public document.

It's crucial that you regard "translating" research for local audiences as a process of making knowledge more accessible, not "dummying it down." Many important public discussions have been derailed because local audiences perceive academic experts as arrogant and remote, a perception that understandably causes resentment and does little to promote cooperation in the public interest. Making specialized knowledge accessible to a non-specialist audience is a sign of courtesy as well as authority. When translating research, try to keep in mind situations in which someone has had to explain unfamiliar information to you—classical music, for example, or the stock market. What strategies did they use to make that information comprehensible and relevant?

While universities contribute to both academic knowledge and local knowledge, they are also geographically specific communities themselves and thus have their own bodies of local knowledge: who the hardest professors are, which computer labs are the least crowded, and so on. Researching the local knowledge of your university can reveal urgent rhetorical situations as well as novel opportunities for intervening in them. While campus directories, catalogs, and newspapers are excellent sources for such knowledge, less prominent university publications (e.g., budgets) and local, state, and national records (e.g., tax returns) can reveal such information as your university's investment portfolio, faculty salaries and research contracts, and campus crime statistics.

Most of this information is fairly easy to find at a public university, and as discussed in Chapter 1, the Freedom of Information Act (FOIA) and other laws guarantee you access to it. If information is seen as politically sensitive, however, you may have difficulty obtaining it. Texts such as *Raising Hell: A Citizen's Guide to the Fine Art of Investigation* and websites like the one sponsored by the Reporters Committee for Freedom of the Press (*http://www.rcfp.org*), can help you to navigate this process successfully.[5]

Local Research in Action

For her local research, Tracy did content analyses of two local newspapers during approximately the same period: the *Wilmington Morning Star*, which is published daily, and the *Wilmington Journal*, a weekly publication with a primarily African-American readership. She wrote down every topic that appeared at least three times during a month, with additional marks for additional mentions. Her lists appear below:

Wilmington Morning Star (April 15–May 15, 2002)

    Terrorism, Sept. 11, war in Afghanistan (too many to count)

    state budget crisis; local programs affected (29)

    Catholic Church sex abuse scandal (17)

    violence in Israel/West Bank (12)

    possibility of raising property taxes to make up for budget cuts (8)

    pollution and global warming (7)

    city-county consolidation (7)

    redistricting (6)

    zoning issues (6)

    foster child missing in Florida (5)

    Jimmy Carter's visit to Cuba (5)

    wildfires in Western U.S. (5)

    School Board debates school uniforms (5)

    middle school trip to Disney World—educational value? (5)

    beach erosion (4); beach safety (4)

    mailbox pipe bomber (4)

    speed humps in local neighborhoods (4)

    state lottery (4)

    Enron/Arthur Andersen trials (4)

    Oklahoma bridge crash (3)

    Chandra Levy investigation (3)

    teen tobacco use (3)

    neglect of drama room at high school (3)

    NC strawberries—in season; some infected with anthracnose which rots them (3)

    need for ESL teachers in county schools (3)

Wilmington Journal (April–May, 2002)

    shortage of minority teachers in county (9)

    Al Sharpton visits, establishes National Action Network (8)

    "driving-while-black" (5)

fair housing issues (5)

alleged incidents of racial discrimination: spitting on teacher's aide (5), jailhouse beating (4), Food Lion hit and run (4), employment bias at hospital (3)

death of [African-American state Senator] Luther Jordan (4)

profiles of candidates for U.S. Senate (4)

NAACP increases membership fees (3)

lack of major accomplishments by NC Black Caucus (3)

jazz legend Percy Heath honored at Walk of Fame (3)

school uniforms (3)

voter fraud investigations in Florida (3)

reparations to ancestors of former slaves (3)

redistricting (3)

black students more likely than white students to be suspended from area schools (3)

activities of Community Action Group (3)

After doing this exercise, Tracy was struck by the fact that the *Journal* and the *Morning Star* published very little of the same news, and when they did, they usually brought radically different perspectives to their articles and editorials. She was particularly disturbed to find that the issue that received the most attention in the *Journal* during the period of her analysis—the shortage of minority teachers in county schools—received absolutely no coverage in the *Morning Star*, and that the issues discussed most frequently in the *Morning Star*—war and national security, the sex abuse scandal in the Catholic Church, and various local government issues—received little or no coverage in the *Journal*. Tracy also noted that each newspaper carried regular columns that the other newspaper did not—one related to religious instruction in the *Journal*, for example. After consulting the original list of interests and concerns that she compiled in her writer's notebook (see Chapter 1), Tracy realized that with the exception of neighborhood traffic problems, none of the issues on her list were represented in either publication.

These observations led Tracy to conclude that the African-American and white populations of Wilmington were sharply divided in terms of what they thought was important and newsworthy. She wondered whether African-American residents feel like they have a stake in local government and whether white residents feel concerned about issues primarily affecting their black neighbors.

Tracy also noticed that the *Wilmington Journal* proclaims on its editorial masthead that it is "Founded on the Principles of the Black Press Creed," which holds that "America can best lead the world away from racial and national antagonisms when it accords to every person, regardless of race, color, or creed, full human and legal rights[, h]ating no person in the firm belief that all are hurt as long as anyone is held back." Since the *Morning Star* avows no such policy, Tracy speculated that the *Journal* might function at least in part as an advocacy publication for the local African-American population.

Taking her cue from *Journal* articles, Tracy decided to set up an interview with a spokesperson for the Community Action Group—a nonpartisan, interracial citizens group that held biweekly forums to discuss local affairs—whom she located simply by consulting the local telephone directory. Among other things, Tracy learned from her interview that many African-American residents of Wilmington subscribe to both the *Morning Star* and the *Journal* because they regard both perspectives as important, but that since the *Journal* operates on a limited budget it can't afford a "newspapers in education" program that places it in the public schools. (It is available locally in all public and academic libraries.)

Reflecting on this information, Tracy recalled a "Politics of Literacy" class in which she learned, among other things, that people become not just literate but also politically conscious through the use of language and concepts that matter in their daily lives—which explained why for some people, the most influential sites of literacy education were churches, prisons, social and civic organizations, therapeutic settings, and family networks rather than schools. Tracy wondered whether the Community Action Group might also function in this way, providing opportunities for African Americans to develop as vital, literate citizens, using the *Wilmington Journal* as a tool.

Tracy was convinced that the discrepancies between local "mainstream" and "black" news suggested several urgent rhetorical situations, including a possible shortage of relevant information and literacy development opportunities for many local residents. She knew, however, that it would be inappropriate to send copies of the readings from her college writing class to the editor of the *Morning Star*. Instead, Tracy listed several other possible actions she might take in order to respond to the situation:

> organize a public roundtable discussion of race and the media
>
> write a letter to the editor of the Morning Star requesting more news coverage relevant to African Americans
>
> picket newspaper offices
>
> raise money to purchase Journal subscriptions for local schools
>
> work with Community Action Group to develop study group

After working through the "Thinking Rhetorically" checklists in Chapters 3 and 4, Tracy decided to pursue the last idea on her list. We'll revisit her efforts in Chapter 7.

Case in Point: Translation

Academic research is not the only kind of knowledge that may require translation in order to be made intelligible to members of a local public. Sometimes the most rudimentary public literacy texts—food labels, W-2 forms, and the like—must be translated into other languages in order to make them accessible to residents. Local governments may take responsibility for these translations, especially when very large numbers of residents speak other languages, as is the case in many big cities. In Winston-Salem, North Carolina, for example, Police Officer Jeff Bloome (with the help of an interpreter) hosts a call-in radio show on the Spanish-language station, Que Pasa Communications. The program was begun as a way to promote clinics on school bus safety and the use of child safety seats; it has since broadened its focus to include traffic laws in general as well as other civil concerns.

Although the Winston-Salem Police Department funds Officer Bloome's program, the burden of this kind of outreach effort usually falls to bilingual volunteers or independent advocacy groups. Amigos International is one such group. This organization was established in Wilmington, North Carolina, in 1998, after Lucy Vasquez discovered that the area's many Hispanic residents (mostly migrant workers) did not understand broadcasts related to hurricane safety and evacuation. Today, Amigos International provides legal aid, information related to immigration and naturalization, referrals for social services, ESL (English as a Second Language) classes, and cultural enrichment programs. It also sponsors the annual Festival Latino and produces a weekly Latino music and current affairs show on the local public radio station.

Most immigrants—particularly those who do not speak English—relocate to an area because people who share their language and culture already live there, often family members or associates from their home country. Usually, some members of these communities have learned enough English through school, work, or the mass media to understand much of what is conveyed through public literacy documents (e.g., procedures for getting a driver's license) and translate this knowledge to their friends and neighbors. In other words, some immigrants, even citizens, are able to live quite comfortably in the the United States without speaking or understanding English; in fact, naturalization ceremonies for new American citizens are often conducted in more than one language. Since this country does not have a national language, these linguistic accommodations are not only sensible but mandated by law.

Language differences do pose problems, however. Many immigrants are isolated from public knowledge and participation because of language difficulties, illiteracy, places of residence, financial circumstances, or fears of deportation, and as a result they may not gain access to needed services such as health care and legal representation—even if such services are available. Although many advocacy groups for non-English-speaking residents have websites promoting their services, other constraints may exist. Members of target populations may not have access to a computer, for example, or they may not be able to read in their own language. They might be mentally ill or have unreliable transportation. How do these members of the public sphere gain access to public literacy?

Of course, non-English speakers are not the only ones who may have limited access to public discourse. People with visual or hearing impairments might experience similar difficulties and similar feelings of isolation. The government (like most businesses) is required to provide "reasonable accommodations" for employees with disabilities, as well as students who attend public schools and residents who are engaged in required government activities—filing income tax forms or serving on a jury, for example. Unfortunately, as suggested in Chapter 4, sometimes groups must pursue legal remedies to their exclusion from public literacy.

Alone or in small groups, brainstorm a list of individuals or groups in your local community who might benefit from the translation of public literacy documents because of language problems or other constraints. Then, using the strategies described in this chapter, research the availability of such services for the groups you identified. You might begin by exploring local government sites or searching for "Hispanic legal services" or "Islamic advocacy organizations" (for example) using a search engine of your choice. As you conduct your research, consider the following questions:

- What public information, if any, is so essential that it must be made available to all members of a local community, regardless of expense or other difficulties and regardless of the audience's legal status? (You may wish to consider the rights of convicted criminals here as well.)

- Whose responsibility is it to translate public information (including public instruction) into languages that non-English speakers (some of whom may be non-citizens or even illegal residents) and disabled people can understand? Why do you think so?

- Since language is only one of many barriers to participating in public literacy, what public spheres besides websites might be effective in getting public information into the hands of people who need it?

If you are not aware of any local individuals or groups who could benefit from a translator or interpreter, research these questions from a different perspective. You may wish to explore them in the context of state or national government or investigate the offerings in a city or state where you know there are many non-English speakers (e.g., Los Angeles). Ask yourself the same questions as you conduct your research.

The presence, absence, or relative convenience of translating services in a local community can say a lot about its values and priorities. Such circumstances can also introduce many opportunities for public literacy. If you believe that your city should devote more resources to the translation of public documents and instruction for the benefit of non-English-speaking or disabled residents—or conversely, if you believe that it should devote *fewer* resources—then you might want to write a letter of concern to the City Council Chairperson or School Superintendant (see Chapter 6), apply for a grant that would fund such efforts (see Chapter 8), or circulate a petition to demonstrate community support for your ideas (see Chapter 9).

Notes

1. Barton, David, and Mary Hamilton. *Local Literacies: Reading and Writing in One Community*. London: Routledge, 1998. Geertz, Clifford. *Local Knowledge: Further Essays in Interpretive Anthropology*. New York: Basic, 1983.

2. Ballenger, Bruce. *The Curious Researcher: A Guide to Writing Research Papers*. 2nd. ed. Boston: Allyn & Bacon, 1998. 204–7.

3. Berendt, John. *Midnight in the Garden of Good and Evil: A Savannah Story*. New York: Random House, 1994. 26, 42.

4. Brown, Cynthia Stokes. *Like It Was: A Complete Guide to Writing Oral History*. New York: Teachers & Writers Collaborative, 1988.

5. Noyes, Dan. *Raising Hell: A Citizen's Guide to the Fine Art of Investigation*. San Francisco: Center for Investigative Reporting, 1983.

CHAPTER 6

Focus on Letters

Letters represent one of the most common public literacy genres—not to mention one of the most versatile. Among other things, letters can express opinions, rally support for an idea, offer praise or censure, ask for money, and request information. Of course, letters serve many other purposes besides public ones (e.g., personal correspondence), and those that appear in the public sphere are not necessarily in the public interest. But their ability to reach a broad audience while still sounding personal makes letters an ideal genre choice for a variety of rhetorical situations.

Ironically, it's because letters are such a familiar genre that some writers have a hard time thinking of them as public literacy texts. While most letters share some basic conventions—a greeting and closing, a signature—the specific content, form, and tone of a letter are determined by its purpose. Although this chapter is not a "how-to" guide, it will sketch the rhetorical contours of four types of letters commonly used for public purposes: letters to editors of publications, letters of concern, appeal letters, and open letters.

Letters to the Editor

Letters to the editor of a publication generally comment on material that appears in that publication. Sometimes these letters add or clarify information or offer a different perspective; in such cases, an urgent rhetorical situation is occasioned by incorrect, biased, or incomplete information. Often, writers use letters to question editorial decisions—some major, some relatively minor. For example, when one local newspaper started running the comic strip *The Boondocks*, many readers protested in the form of letters to the editor, and the strip was briefly pulled before an additional round of letters brought about its reinstatement. In these cases, the rhetorical situation is considered urgent because of a perceived lapse in editorial judgment that writers regard as correctable through discourse.

Some letters to the editor might be more accurately described as letters to *readers* of a publication. For example, in some local newspapers it's not unusual to read a letter like this one: "The Max Garratt who was arrested for drunk driving on March 1 was not the Max Garratt who owns Garratt's Print Shop." In this case, it was readers of the newspaper, not editors, who composed the rhetorical audience—that is, the audience capable of acting on the information in the letter (e.g., by continuing to patronize Mr. Garratt's business). The editors are also a rhetorical audience in this situation, however: as the *gatekeepers* of the public interest, it was they who decided to publish the letter (and of course, as local citizens, they can also choose whether to support Garratt's Print Shop).

It can be useful when writing a letter to the editor to mention any special experience or credentials that make you an expert on the issue you are addressing. Sometimes, though, this information reveals possible conflicts of interest. For example, a self-identified physician wrote a letter to the editor of a magazine in response to an article on the popularity of alternative healing methods such as acupuncture. She compared practitioners of these methods to snake-oil salesmen and urged readers to consult medical doctors for serious health problems. Certainly, this doctor's education and professional experience give her some amount of authority on this subject, and indeed, she might have felt ethically obligated to express her professional opinion in this situation. But she might also have a financial stake in steering readers away from alternative healers, a possibility which somewhat undermines her message.

Most letters columns feature submission guidelines, including recommended length, postal and e-mail addresses, and so on. These guidelines may constrain your writing to some extent, but it is wise to follow them carefully, for letters that don't meet the guidelines might be summarily rejected, regardless of the content. If a letter is too long to publish, the editors might revise it themselves, in which case you run the risk of having your ideas distorted or important information deleted.

When you submit a letter to the editor, you are usually required not only to sign your name but also to include your address and phone number so that the editorial staff can verify that you wrote the letter before they publish it. This practice exists primarily to hold writers accountable for the opinions they express publicly. If people were not required to sign their names, they would be free to make outrageous or inaccurate claims—anonymously or in someone else's name.

The features of a good letter to the editor vary widely, which is why you should always look at letters columns in target publications for models. In general, though, letters should address a matter in the public interest, assert a clear point, communicate that point accurately and concisely, and convey a calm, sensible tone. They should demonstrate understanding and respect for the cultural and educational sensibilities of readers and avoid insulting or inflammatory language, name-calling, and intentional deception. Finally, they should be conscientiously revised and edited. Your letter might still be published even if it doesn't meet these criteria, but it has a better chance of influencing both editors and readers if it does.

Exercise

Find letters columns in several of the following kinds of publications: student newspaper, local daily or weekly newspaper, national newspaper (e.g., USA *Today*), weekly or monthly general interest magazine (e.g., *TIME*, *Smithsonian*), popular culture magazine (e.g., *People*), special interest magazine or newspaper (e.g., *Outside*, *Baseball Weekly*), academic journal, and on-line magazine (e.g., *Slate*).

Then, alone or in small groups, compare and contrast the submission guidelines for each publication and the characteristics of the letters they publish. What accounts for these similarities and differences? Are there some letters that seem "better" than others? If so, why?

Newspapers and magazines suggest innumerable rhetorical situations. Some may inspire you to write letters to the editor, but others may inform you of urgent situations that you could respond to through other public literacy genres or actions. Challenge yourself to read a local or national newspaper several times a week, paying special attention to those moments where you find yourself thinking, "That's not fair!" or "Somebody should do something about that." Record potential rhetorical situations in your writer's notebook.

Letters of Concern

Letters of concern are generally directed toward individuals for the purpose of seeking assistance, improving a situation, or solving a problem. What distinguishes them from letters of *complaint* is that they try to propose actions or solutions rather than simply identify problems. Of course, sometimes we experience urgent problems that we don't know how to solve. Often, though, we know how our situations could be improved but just need to forward our ideas to a rhetorical audience—that is, a person or persons capable of carrying them out.

Because letters of concern are generally sent to individuals, they aren't "public" in the sense that all members of a national, local, global, or everyday public have access to them as *readers*. However, such letters often address issues in the public interest, and the genre is available to all members of a public as *writers*. Public officials often make good rhetorical audiences; as discussed in Chapter 5, their contact information is readily available on-line, at libraries, and in the phone book.

Like letters to the editor, letters of concern are more likely to reach their intended audience if they conform to certain basic conventions. Since traditional business letters are among the most formal of letter genres, they can convey the seriousness of your concern as well as invoke an audience who takes your ideas seriously.

Although there are many different kinds of business letters, they are generally brief (ideally, no more than one page) and get to the point quickly; they specify problems and solutions directly, and establish the writer's relationship to the recipient (including the recipient's obligations, if any, to the writer) at the outset. The tone of a letter of concern should be polite but earnest. As with letters to the editor, the writer should make every effort to provide accurate, relevant information, and be mindful of the interests of their audience.

Business letter format varies widely as well, but the most formal are written in "block style" (left margins flush, no indentations) and include these features:

Date: month (spelled out), day, year

Address: the same one that appears on the envelope, including recipient's name and appropriate title of office (e.g., Dr. Carol Cullum, Vice President of Student Development)

Greeting: "Dear ——" (title and last name) followed by a colon; letters of complaint should ideally be directed toward a specific person, but if this is not possible, use a generic description such as "Dear Vice President"

Body: short paragraphs, with a space between each paragraph
> *first paragraph* (1–2 sentences): establishes relationship to recipient and purpose for writing
> *middle paragraphs*: elaborates on request (e.g., by providing evidence of problem, and describing prior efforts to seek assistance and possible benefits of proposed actions)
> *final paragraph* (1–2 sentences): reiterates the urgency of the situation and asks recipient to take specific action

Closing: "Yours truly" or some similar phrase, followed by a comma

Signature: your name, signed in ink; leave three lines between closing and your typewritten name

Enclosures: "encl."; an optional feature which indicates that additional materials (e.g., receipts) are included with your letter

Copies: "cc" followed by a colon and names of any other recipients, listed in alphabetical order; optional

These conventions can be adapted to meet the needs of less formal rhetorical situations—for example, by indenting paragraphs and moving the date and closing to the right (see "Appeal Letters" below).

Exercise

Look through the problems and concerns you have listed in your writer's notebook and select one or two that seem particularly important to you. Then, brainstorm several possible solutions or improvements and several rhetorical audiences to whom you might address letters of concern. If the rhetorical situation is urgent and a letter of concern seems like an appropriate genre with which to respond to it, write your letter, ask a partner to read it with an eye toward possible revisions, and send it.

Below you will see the letter that Debbie drafted to send to the Vice President of Student Development at her community college, expressing her concerns about the harassment of women who breastfeed in public and proposing local remedies to the problem as she experienced it. Although initially uncertain whether this represented an issue in the public interest, Debbie was convinced that she should pursue her efforts when she noticed that many of the state laws that protect the rights of nursing mothers emphasize the public health benefits of breastfeeding.

Consult the criteria for effective letters of concern and the peer review questions listed at the end of this chapter, then read Debbie's letter carefully. What suggestions would you offer Debbie as she undertakes her revisions?

March 28, 2002

Carol Cullum
Vice President of Student Development
Cape Fear Community College
411 N. Front St.
Wilmington, NC 28401

Dear Dr. Cullum:

I am a student at Cape Fear Community College and I am writing to complain about being harassed by a campus security officer even though I was not engaged in any illegal behavior.

On Wednesday, March 27, at approximately 5:45 p.m., I was discreetly breastfeeding my son on a 2nd floor bench in the McLeod Building before my 6:30 class. Officer Roger Daye requested several times that I move. I refused. He left, but returned a few minutes later accompanied by a female security officer. Officer Daye directed that she take down my name. I gave my name but chose to remain seated where I was, nursing my child.

Officer Daye stated that my breastfeeding in public was "obscene" and that my refusal to leave was disruptive. However, breastfeeding in public is protected by state law. Section 1.G.S. 4-190.9 of the North Carolina General Statutes says that "a woman may breastfeed in any public or private location where she is otherwise authorized to be, irrespective of whether the nipple of the mother's breast is uncovered during or incidental to the breast feeding." Many states have adopted laws like this because they recognize the health benefits of breastfeeding and want to do all they can to support it.

I don't know how common my experience is, but I do know that CFCC has many older students like myself, and many of us have young children. As the Vice President of Student Development, I am sure that you will want to take steps to make our campus safe and comfortable for all students and to make sure our legal rights are protected. At minimum, security guards must be educated about these rights. In addition, it might be a good idea for the school to make private rooms (for example, study rooms at the library) available for mothers who are embarrassed to nurse in public.

Thank you for your attention to this issue. I look forward to hearing from you.

Sincerely,

Debbie Asberry

Debbie received a letter of apology from the Vice President of her college, who thanked her for the information she provided and assured her that security personnel would be apprised of the legal rights of nursing mothers. Debbie's story does not end there, however. Before composing her letter, Debbie contacted a lactation consultant with the local chapter of La Leche League International, an advocacy and support organization for nursing mothers; it was the consultant, in fact, who advised Debbie of her legal rights and urged her to consult the group's website for additional information. At the next League meeting, the lactation consultant distributed what appeared to be business cards and said, "If you're ever hassled about breastfeeding in public, just pull this out." The cards summarized the state statutes that guarantee women the right to breastfeed in public.

The cards are noteworthy for at least two reasons. For one, they represent a public literacy document so specific to a set of rhetorical circumstances as to defy genre classification. For another, they exemplify the process by which public literacy texts generate other public literacy texts: one document leads to another and then another, and before long writers find themselves participating in a lively public conversation.

Appeal Letters

Appeal letters are sent to mass audiences on behalf of individuals or organizations. Because their purpose is usually to raise money or rally support for a cause, they are often used by political candidates or parties and by nonprofit groups like the Humane Society or the Cystic Fibrosis Foundation. Appeal letters should be distinguished from *solicitation* letters, such as credit card or magazine subscription offers, whose purpose is primarily to make money rather than promote some public interest.

Appeal letters usually arrive in the mail and may include a postage-paid return envelope. But there are other ways of sending appeal letters, too. For example, groups like the Surfrider Foundation, which is devoted to beach conservation and water quality monitoring, rely on e-mail distribution lists to send appeal letters at no cost; their website also allows supporters to charge donations on a credit card. The advantage of these strategies is that they save time and resources—which is important for non-profit organizations operating on tight budgets, particularly environmental groups that don't want to appear to be wasting the very resources they seek to preserve. One down side of electronic appeal letters is that they are not accessible to potential supporters who don't have computers or Internet access, which is why the Surfriders and most other groups also send appeal letters via "snail mail."

Another disadvantage of electronic appeal letters is that they may be presumed to be hoaxes. In recent years, e-mail users have been inundated with messages from writers pleading for money for purposes that sound noble but are in fact fraudulent. One such example is written by someone claiming to be an exiled African prince whose assets have been frozen. He needs money deposited *immediately* in an offshore bank account so that he can reclaim his position and initiate democratic political reforms—all you have to do is send him your credit card number! The message is usually personalized and riddled with the kinds of language and editorial errors that a non-English speaker might make. And while sophisticated readers might see right through the scam, this kind of unscrupulous use of electronic media has made potential donors rightfully wary of even the most worthy on-line financial appeals.

Most appeal letters are sponsored by some larger organization, such as a nonprofit agency, and therefore represent national, global, or local public literacies. Sometimes, though, appeal letters take the form of everyday public literacies. Such letters might be published in a church newsletter, on flyers posted around town or tucked in mailboxes, or on e-mail (as with James and Chandler's efforts to promote their Yellow Bike program, discussed in Chapter 4). Everyday appeal letters are usually inspired by specific events rather than ongoing membership drives or fundraising efforts. Examples include documents requesting donations of household goods for a congregation member whose home was destroyed in a fire, contributions to Toys for Tots, or assistance in finding a lost pet.

The content and form of everyday appeal letters is fairly flexible. However, most organizations want to give the impression that their issue is so urgent that they don't have time to write formal letters. To achieve this goal, they often adapt standard business letter format in order to make their appeal letters appear hastily composed—for example, by using a comma after the greeting and closing, indenting paragraphs, omitting the date, and making liberal use of exclamation marks and ellipses (. . .). Appeal letters might further deviate from formal business letter conventions by printing photographs directly onto the page, using computer fonts that resemble handwriting, extending their message over several pages, and running their address across the bottom of the first page. Many add a "P.S." at the end or affix simulated "post-its."

Most organizations purchase mailing lists from other sources that share similar ideals or constituencies—veterans' advocacy groups, for example, might buy addresses from the American Association for Retired Persons (AARP), or vice versa. While this practice might assist groups in reaching a large and receptive audience, it can also have the opposite effect. Some people receive so many appeal letters that they can't distinguish one group's "urgent" needs from those of another; feeling overwhelmed, these potential members of a rhetorical audience may simply discard appeal letters without reading them.

The lesson here is that audiences for appeal letters should be chosen carefully. While you want to reach many people efficiently, you also want to ensure that your letter will actually be read. In general, readers are more receptive to letters that *ap-*

pear to be written to them personally, even if they know this isn't the case. If you received three appeal letters from organizations whose interests you shared, which would you be most inclined to read further: the one that begins "To Our Friends at 5310 Clear Run Drive," the one that begins "Dear American Patriot," or the one that greets you by name?

Computer programs can assist you in customizing appeal letters sent to mass audiences. It's worth remembering, though, that some people regard appeal letters as the public literacy equivalent of telemarketing and thus simply refuse to read them, regardless of how personal they appear. This constraint can make appeal letters a risky genre choice.

Because they are usually asking people to give support or even money, it is common for appeal letters to resort to extreme emotional tactics, including shocking pictures or stories, to demonstrate the urgency of their cause. These messages might even appear on the envelope, such as this one from an international children's advocacy organization:

HANDLE WITH CARE
HEAT & WATER
MAY CAUSE SEVERE
DAMAGE

URGENT: OPEN IMMEDIATELY

Donald Bushman
1104 University
Dixon, IL 61021

The envelope contained some complimentary cabbage seeds, and next to a picture of a severely malnourished child, the letter read, in part: "Hold the packet of seeds as you look at this little child—you are holding his life in your hands!!"

Although the organization's goals might be worthy and its letter's claims accurate, you should be critical of such tactics as a reader; and although they can be very effective, you should use them sparingly as a writer. If you ever work for a nonprofit agency or political party—as an employee or a volunteer—you may be asked to draft an appeal letter. While the use of emotionalism might be appropriate in such letters, it is essential that your information be completely accurate in order to maintain your own credibility and that of your organization.

Exercise

Collect several examples of national, local, global, and everyday appeal letters and examine them in small groups. What common features do they share? What, if anything, distinguishes one from another? How would you characterize the language and tone of the letters? After reading their letters, are you interested in supporting any of these organizations or efforts? Why or why not?

Open Letters

Open letters are typically placed by individuals or special interest groups in local or national publications for the purpose of invoking the support of a receptive audience. In most cases, they are used to clarify information; express apologies, explanations, disapproval, or gratitude; ask for support; or outline a political agenda.

Sometimes open letters take the form of editorials that are written by columnists for publication in local or national periodicals. Often, though, they are simply paid advertisements or public relations efforts that resemble personal letters, business memos, or news items. Such constraints tend to limit this genre—at least at the local and national levels—to professional writers and individuals or groups who can afford to buy advertising space. Even though open letters may address issues in the public interest, it is a good idea to read their claims critically, as you would a television commercial or political advertisement, for evidence of bias or self interest.

Even if they do not use traditional business letter format, many open letters—like the following one from Unidad Cubana—are published on the official letterhead of an office or organization. And while this letter doesn't include a formal greeting, closing, or actual signatures, it purposefully evokes these conventions. On the surface, the letter appears only to articulate its positions on various aspects of American foreign policy affecting Cuba. However, by publishing its letter in the *Washington Monthly*—whose readers include politicians, political staff members, and private citizens capable of influencing the actions of politicians—the organization is also soliciting the support and political advocacy of its audience.

Open letters that appear in everyday public spheres typically do not represent advertising. On a grocery store bulletin board, you might see a notice thanking area residents for helping find a lost cat. When the town of Show Low, Arizona, was spared destruction from an approaching forest fire in 2002, the national news showed a family who had painted a message on the roof of their home thanking firefighters for their assistance. Although not all everyday open letters express gratitude, their purposes are usually to maintain interpersonal relationships and reinforce community values, not promote a special interest.

OPEN LETTER TO THE PRESIDENT AND THE CONGRESS OF THE UNITED STATES

A STATEMENT BY UNIDAD CUBANA

*"There is a limit to the tears shed over the graves of the dead,
and that is the infinite love of the Country that is sworn over their dead bodies."* — José Martí

Unidad Cubana publicly reaffirms the position it has been stating since its foundation on July 12, 1991, at Miami's Dade County Auditorium, when nearly all of the organizations and umbrella groups of Cuban exiles agreed that the only solution to the Cuban crisis was to face up to and overthrow the Castro regime.

Therefore, in view of the confusion that some of the exile organizations have created by changing this stand, Unidad Cubana, made up of dozens of organizations, reaffirms:

1) That in Cuba nothing has changed to justify trying to alter or change the policy on which Unidad Cubana labored along with other organizations and with our Congressmen in Washington, D.C., for the passing of the Helms-Burton Act.

2) That Unidad Cubana expresses that, in essence, nothing has changed in Cuba after the Pope's visit, even though some of those who seek an "understanding" with the Communist tyranny claim otherwise in order to weaken the U.S. embargo and create a false notion about the nature of the Castro regime.

3) That we continue to wholeheartedly support our Members of Congress, Ilenna Ros-Lehtinen, Lincoln Díaz-Balart, and Bob Menéndez, whom we consider our voices in Washington, D.C., and to whom, therefore, we offer all the cooperation they need and is within our means to continue their patriotic struggle.

4) That we do not accept a solution based on the so-called "socialist laws" whereby those who are responsible for the destruction inflicted upon Cuba would be allowed to remain in power.

5) That Unidad Cubana, as an umbrella organization consisting of many member groups, respects their respective points of view as long as none of these is based on a dialog or *detente* with the tyranny.

6) That, just as we shall continue to help the dissident groups and the independent press, as well as those patriots who are waging war on the regime inside Cuba, we shall also continue to mobilize internationally to denounce those who would take over the resources stolen from Cuban and foreign citizens. Once Cuba is free of Castroism, we shall take these unscrupulous usurpers to court and force them to pay the appropriate reparations for their collaboration with Castro's totalitarian regime.

7) That we urge all those who agree with the total liberation of Cuba, and with the indictment of the criminals, to add their signatures to this Statement and join Unidad Cubana to help accomplish its high goals. Please call us at (305) 649-6950.

8) The leaders of Unidad Cubana reiterate their commitment to our country, to the people inside Cuba, and to the Cubans in exile, in order to achieve what those who have died on the altar of the Fatherland, the political prisoners, and those who chose the bitter path of exile, have been fighting for over the best years of their lives.

9) The only *Magna Carta* recognized by Unidad Cubana is the Constitution of 1940, which contains all the democratic elements that are needed for the reconstruction of Cuba.

10) Unidad Cubana wishes to take advantage of this opportunity to express its disagreement with the recent policy announced by the President of the United States in regard to Cuba. We feel that the almost 40 years of the Castro regime's inflexible totalitarian policy is more than sufficient to demonstrate that Fidel Castro will not change this policy because the U.S. government allows humanitarian aid to Cuba or direct flights to that country. Among many other things that we could state is the fact that this weak policy of opening to Castro without Castro making a single move concerning the respect of human rights in Cuba or its democratization, shows the dictator that to obtain concessions from the United States what he has to do is to continue oppressing the Cuban people.

Signed in Miami, Florida, U.S.A., in March, 1998, and read in a room of the Congress of the United States before Members of Congress friendly to Cuba's freedom, and the leadership of the Unidad Cubana.

P.O. BOX 1973 / MIAMI, FL 33135 • 807 S.W. 25 AVE. / OFICINA 209 / MIAMI, FL 33135 • TELEFONO: (305) 649-6950 • FAX: (305) 649-7054

Figure 6.1. Individuals or organizations must usually pay to publish open letters like this one, which appeared in *Washington Monthly*. Such documents may represent a form of advertising or public relations and should be scrutinized carefully for possible conflicts of interest.[1]

There are, of course, exceptions and ambiguities. For example, a local hot dog vendor whose business permit was revoked for health violations erected a sandwich board near his establishment; titled "An Open Letter to New Hanover County Commissioners," the document alleged a variety of unfair administrative practices that adversely affected local small business owners like himself. Whether the vendor's open letter was in the public interest or his own self interest is debatable, but his claims did reach a rhetorical audience who contacted the County Commissioners on his behalf.

As these examples illustrate, most open letters are addressed to individuals in positions of power—the President, for example, or County Commissioners. Of course it would have been possible (and certainly cheaper) for members of Unidad Cubana to write letters of concern to the President expressing identical sentiments. But open letters are not just addressed to their recipients; they are also addressed to an audience of "witnesses"—that is, people who can hold the recipient accountable to receiving and acting on a message. By addressing the President "in front of" the readership of the *Washington Monthly*, for example, Unidad Cubana is also trying to persuade other people to accept their arguments and put pressure on the President to accept them as well. If a single individual or a small, inaccessible committee has the power to take action on your behalf but you are concerned that your communication with them will be lost or ignored, then an open letter might be a smart genre choice.

The form of an open letter will be dictated primarily by the public sphere in which it is published. Particularly if you are paying for advertising space, you want your letter to be as correct and professional looking as possible; you may wish to examine other examples of open letters as models or consult an advertising agent at your target publication. As a general rule, audiences are more willing to overlook editing errors if you are thanking or praising them for something or if the document is clearly informal and expects nothing but goodwill from its audience.

The most important criteria for evaluating an open letter, or for deciding whether you should write one yourself, are whether it addresses an issue that is legitimately in the public interest and which public sphere is most accessible to a rhetorical audience.

Exercise

Search an electronic database like EBSCOhost or Lexis-Nexis using the keyword *open letter*. Although you can probably read the texts on-line, track down several of the citations at your campus or local library so that you can see the letters in their original form. Compare and contrast several examples. In general, what kinds of rhetorical situations do open letters respond to?

Look through your writer's notebook. Can you find any rhetorical situations for which an open letter might be an appropriate response? (Remember, your decision will depend heavily on the rhetorical audience.)

Open letters that are treated by newspapers as paid advertisements typically do not show up in electronic databases. They may, however, be referred to in editorials or news items, so you should make sure that your database searches not only titles and abstracts but also the full texts of articles. In 2002, for example, Cardinal Roger Mahony, head of the largest Roman Catholic diocese in the United States, placed open letters in three Los Angeles newspapers to reassure the public that he was doing all he could to prevent future abuse by priests. The letter itself was not archived, but articles *about* the letter were, and these database "hits" made it possible to locate this important document.

Peer Review

Before writing a letter in the public interest, you should work through the "Thinking Rhetorically" checklists in Chapters 3 and 4 to make sure that this is an appropriate response to an urgent rhetorical situation. Before submitting your letter, you should ask someone you trust to read it with the following questions in mind:

- What is the purpose of this letter? Does it clearly and concisely identify the problem and explain why the writer finds this situation urgent? Does it request a specific, feasible action?

- Does the letter address or invoke an appropriate rhetorical audience? Is the writer's relationship to the recipient clearly specified or implied?

- Is the letter respectful of the audience's intelligence and values? Does it include accurate information, with a minimum of emotional appeals?

- How would you characterize the language, tone, and style of the letter? Are these appropriate to the letter's audience and purpose?

- In the case of letters to the editor, does the draft conform to the editorial guidelines described in the target publication?

- In the case of other letters, does the draft conform to or appropriately modify standard business letter format?

- In the case of appeal letters, does the draft identify its sponsor? Does the sponsoring individual or group sound credible?

- After reading the letter, are you inclined to accept the writer's perspective or take the action he/she proposes? Why or why not?

- Is there anything in the letter that strikes you as especially wrong, uninformed, inappropriate, offensive, or suspect? If so, what?

- If there are any problems, how might they be addressed in a revision?

Note

1. *Washington Monthly*. May 1998: 45.

CHAPTER 7

Focus on Media Releases, Media Kits, and Press Conferences

Working with the media is an inevitable part of public literacy. And while the idea of publicity might seem more common among professional marketers, politicians, or celebrities—people promoting a new product or trying to get elected to office—it can also be used by non-professionals to persuade audiences that a rhetorical situation is urgent and demands their immediate action. Writing media releases, compiling media kits, and arranging press conferences all represent ways to facilitate media coverage of an event; they allow you or your group to create a news story that represents *your* perspective and *your* agenda.

Until recently, the genres discussed in this chapter were known exclusively as *press releases* and *press kits*, reflecting their primary function: to communicate, in writing and on paper, with journalists who represented the print media. Although still used widely, these terms are gradually being replaced by *media release* and *media kits*. This new terminology has evolved in tandem with new technologies—including websites and downloadable digital files—which have in turn spawned new audiences, new media outlets, and new purposes for public literacy. Press conferences represent an exception to this trend. As their name implies, they are reserved for members of the traditional news media (and invited guests) and therefore remain a relatively inaccessible forum for communicating the public interest.

Some of the new media outlets differ from their print-based predecessors principally in the platform by which they deliver their information: they are staffed mainly by professional journalists, define "news" in conventional ways, and provide a convenient alternative to newspapers or television newscasts. Other media outlets, however, have been created by amateur activists, commentators, and muckrakers—as well as non-profit groups—who have assumed responsibility for making information available to constituencies underserved by the mainstream media. These individuals and groups and the tools they employ constitute a radically different kind of media—one that has democratized the otherwise restricted genres of press releases and press kits.

Terminology aside, the one thing that hasn't changed about media releases, media kits, and press conferences is their emphasis on clear, concise, action-oriented writing. This chapter will address each of these genres in turn, offering general guidelines about how to write and adapt them effectively.

Media Releases

The basic purpose of a *media release* (also called a *press release* or *news release*) is to announce something—an event, the results of a study, a major accomplishment or undertaking—in a way that attracts positive public attention, or publicity. The media releases you are most likely to write are those that address a lack of media attention to an issue in the public interest. In such cases, media releases can actually "create" news by invoking an audience who cares about what you have to say. When the mainstream local newspaper in Wilmington did not report racial imbalances among county school teachers, for example (see Chapter 5), concerned citizens might have been able to publicize the information through a media release.

As with any rhetorical situation, your media release must address or invoke an audience who can act on your document. Since the first goal is to get your media release published, the most important rhetorical audience is initially the gatekeeper: the person who reads the release and decides whether to reject it or accept it and thus whether to make it accessible to a wider public. Understanding local knowledge can help you to anticipate the biases or interests of specific gatekeepers as well as the kinds of issues that local public audiences tend to respond to.

Major media outlets such as television studios and newspapers receive many media releases every day. Therefore the format and style of your release can be as important as the content. Although these conventions vary slightly, adhering to them will enhance your credibility and increase the likelihood that your release will get careful consideration.

Your first step is to design media release *letterhead* for your organization or concern: stationery that includes the name or logo of your group, as well as its address and phone number, followed by the words "Media Release" or "Press Release." (Both legal and letter-sized paper are appropriate for letterhead.) If you send your media releases by post, you should enclose them in envelopes matching the letterhead in style, ink color, and paper color; especially urgent media releases may also be sent by fax or e-mail. Many organizations post and archive media releases on their websites so that interested audiences—including but not limited to members of the media—can stay informed of their activities. In general, these on-line media releases observe the same conventions of traditional hard copy releases.

At the left of your release, underneath the letterhead, you should type "For Release: Immediate" or "For Release: [Date]." If you don't want the information released until a specific date and time, type "Embargoed for Release Until [Date and Time]." Directly across from this information, type "Contact:" and then the name and phone number of the person who can answer questions about the information (usually the person who writes the release).

The content of press releases is generally single-spaced, with double spaces between paragraphs. The basic format of a press release includes these features:

Slug: the title or headline typed in all capital letters and/or bold; briefly summarizes the content of the release, using action verbs to sound as interesting and newsworthy as possible

Lead: the first paragraph (1–2 sentences); answers who, what, when, where, and why, as well as so what? and who cares?

Body: adheres to an "inverted triangle" style, in which the most important information appears first, then slightly less important information, and so on; time constraints may force editors to read only the first few lines of media releases before making a decision whether to use them, and space constraints may force them to delete part of a release, so it's important that all necessary information be immediately accessible

The style of a media release should be short, succinct, and specific; use exact names and dates whenever possible, and make sure your information is completely accurate. Media releases should communicate factual information; they are not editorials. Therefore opinions should either be conveyed through documented quotations or omitted altogether.

In those instances that releases extend beyond one page, type "(more)" at the center bottom of any page that is not your last page. Centered at the bottom of the last page, type "###" or "–30–" to indicate the end of the release. (Both proofreading symbols are acceptable but "–30–" is somewhat outdated.)

Most media releases are directed to national, global, or local publics—the audiences of media outlets. But it's also possible to use writing to release information to everyday publics. If, for example, you wanted to remind your neighbors to attend the annual block party, you might distribute flyers in mailboxes; if you wanted to announce the winners of your residence hall's elections, you might write an informal media release for the hall newsletter or simply create a congratulatory poster. In such situations, "media" release might be something of a misnomer, since the announcements are not mediated by a gatekeeper or other member of the media.

united students against sweatshops

1015 18th street nw, suite 200 . washington dc 20036 . 202 NO SWEAT . www.usasnet.org

FOR IMMEDIATE RELEASE   CONTACT:
THURSDAY, OCTOBER 11, 2001   Evelyn Zepeda: (909) 607-7630
                                Marie Joseph: (607) 257-4178
                                Dale Weaver: (408) 504-5504
                                National Staff: (202) NOSWEAT

Student Support on U.S. Campuses for Workers at Nike/Reebok Factory in Mexico Helps Secure Unprecedented Union Victory

WORKERS WHO MAKE SWEATSHIRTS FOR MAJOR UNIVERSITIES WIN RIGHT TO ORGANIZE

"An independent union for workers at the Mexmode (formerly Kukdong International-Mexico) apparel factory, a Nike/Reebok contractor, has become a reality not only because of the determination of the workers in Mexico but also because of the intense pressure exerted by students and their administrators, an investigation of worker complaints by the Worker Rights Consortium to which 86 US colleges and universities are affiliated, as well as the hard work of other labor rights organizations," said **Marie-Louise Joseph**, a Cornell University student and member of United Students Against Sweatshops.

"The combined solidarity effort helped the workers, who make the sweatshirts many of us wear win an unprecedented victory. It is customary in Mexico for owners of *maquiladora* (export factories) to seek out a contract with a *charro* (protection union), without the consent of the workforce and often before the workers have even been hired, said **Evelyn Zepeda**, a student at Pitzer College and member of United Students Against Sweatshops. "This is the first time in a Mexican maquiladora that workers have been able to get rid of a protection union and replace it with a democratic union of their own choosing," she added.

Over a year and a half ago, United Students Against Sweatshops (USAS), an organization of of student labor rights groups on 175 campuses, began pressing for university action to bring conditions at the Korean-owned Nike/Reebok supplier factory in line with university codes of conduct. Mexmode manufactures sweatshirts bearing college logos for Nike, which supplied them to over a dozen major universities. A delegation of USAS members from ten US campuses met with Mexmode apparel workers in Atlixco, in the Mexican state of Puebla, in December, 2000 to hear about conditions at the plant. In January, 2001, over 800 workers held a three-day work stoppage to protest substandard wages, forced overtime, verbal and physical abuse, sexual harassment, contaminated food, the presence of a corrupt and unrepresentative "protection" union, and the firing of leaders of an independent union organizing effort. Mexmode immediately fired all of the workers and Mexican riot police severely beat many of the workers.

Student protests on over 20 US campuses called on university administrators to intervene with Nike and Reebok to ensure that their supplier rehired the workers without reprisal and recognized the workers' right to choose their own union. Mexmode had signed a contract with a company union even before it hired its first workers. The Worker Rights Consortium (WRC) responded to Mexmode workers' complaints by sending a team of experts in Mexican and international labor law to Atlixco to investigate. The WRC issued a report that found serious violations of university and Nike codes of conduct as well as Mexican and international labor laws and recommended that administrators work with Nike and Reebok to remedy the situation.

Figure 7.1. This media release illustrates several minor modifications of conventional media release format.

WESTWOOD Neighborhood NEWS

Notice of Public Hearing

Your comments are invited on the proposed...

Westwood/Highland Park Neighborhood Plan

and the Mayor's Proposed Response to the Plan

The Seattle City Council will hold a presentation and public hearing

Thursday, June 10, 1999
Presentation: 6:00 p.m. - Public Hearing: 7:00 p.m.
Highland Park United Methodist Church
Fellowship Hall
9001 9th Ave SW (entrance on 10th Ave)

Information about the plan and a sign- up sheet for those wishing to testify will be available at 6:00 p.m.

The proposed Westwood/Highland Park Neighborhood Plan was developed by citizen volunteers working together to enhance and preserve existing natural resources, strengthen connections between the community, preserve existing single family areas, improve multi-family areas, improve transportation and strengthen the neighborhood's economic core. The Mayor's proposed response includes:

* a resolution recognizing the plan and approving a work program for the City to begin implementing portions of the plan; and
* an ordinance with amendments to the City of Seattle's 20-year Comprehensive Plan and amendments to the Seattle Land Use Code.

Figure 7.2. This media release was published in a neighborhood newsletter. As an everyday public literacy document, it is less constrained by conventions regulating format and style.

Writing a media release allows you to control the telling of your story, which can be especially important when announcing bad news. Most media outlets welcome well-written releases and may even read or publish them verbatim. If this happens, then your media release has been successful. However, if *you* can reap the benefits of a cooperative media, then so can individuals or groups that are *not* acting in the public interest. It's important, therefore, to think critically about what the media publishes as news—that is, to consider who wrote it and whose interests it represents.

Exercise

In your writer's notebook, make a list of projects you are currently involved in and significant developments in your life. This list might include a research paper you're working on, an upcoming trip, a new relationship . . . anything at all that's interesting or important to you. Then, choose one item from your list and write a media release announcing it. Remember, many media releases are designed to promote "soft" news that the media would not otherwise cover, so you need to make them sound as urgent as possible and attend carefully to format and style conventions.

Media Kits

The basic purpose of a *media kit* is to help the media cover an event or news story. The more information journalists have at their fingertips, the less work they will have to do in terms of double-checking facts, interviewing sources, and so on, and the more likely they will be to give favorable media coverage to a matter you or your group finds urgent. As with media releases, the most important audience for a media kit is the representative of a media outlet who decides whether the information is newsworthy. A good media kit should make the gatekeeper's decision as easy as possible.

Media kits are helpful when a rhetorical situation is complicated or involves several parties—that is, when there are multiple opportunities for confusion, such as misspelling names or misunderstanding key information. Let's say, for example, that you are holding a press conference to announce the results of a study jointly sponsored by three organizations for the purpose of documenting wheelchair access to public buildings in your community. A media kit might include a press release announcing the results of the study, a copy of the study itself, informational brochures related to the sponsoring agencies, and copies of any laws or ordinances related to disability access.

The traditional media kit assembles a media release and a few other documents, called *attachments*, in a pocketed "presentation folder," which may feature a group's name or logo. More innovative media kits might be distributed via a CD-ROM or website; while they typically include digitized versions of conventional print sources, they are just as likely to feature downloadable graphics, video or audio files or streams, and links to other sites.

Common examples of attachments include the following:

"backgrounders" or fact sheets	mission statements
FAQs (frequently asked questions)	calendars or schedules of events
copies of or links to relevant media coverage	budgets and timetables
list of photo or interview opportunities	maps or floor plans
promotional flyers or brochures or links to affiliate organizations	
photographs (with captions), videotapes or files, graphics	
biographical sketches of people mentioned prominently in media release	

Of course, too much information can overwhelm an audience, so you probably wouldn't include all of these items in your media kit. Likewise, you can surely think of many other documents that could be appropriate. The choice of attachments depends on your goals and the rhetorical situation.

You may decide to include in your media kit attachments written for other purposes (e.g., your organization's mission statement) or even appropriated from other sources (e.g., research reports, news coverage). This is generally acceptable as long as you document your sources carefully (somebody researched and wrote each of those texts, after all) and include an adequate number of attachments that were prepared specifically in response to the present rhetorical situation. As with all public documents, your media kit needs to convey the urgency of the rhetorical situation; if it depends too heavily on "recycled" material, the event or information you are announcing may seem stale, hence not newsworthy.

When arranging a media kit in a presentation folder, always place the two most important documents at the front of the pocket on each side of the folder; one of these is usually the media release. Arrange additional documents behind these, in the order in which you want your audience to see them. You might want to attach a cover letter to the front of the folder describing the contents of the media kit and, if applicable, an agenda for the press conference. It is, of course, more difficult to direct the audience's reading patterns with media kits presented in electronic formats. Nevertheless, you should still make an effort to clearly organize and label your information so that readers can easily find not only what they are looking for but also what you or your group consider most important.

The format and presentation of your media kit are constrained primarily by its purpose and content but also by your budget. If you are promoting soft news, such as a beach carnival to raise money for Special Olympics, you might put the contents of your media kit in a plastic bucket or include a carnival token. This kind of packaging wouldn't detract from the message and might even enhance it. If, on the other hand, you are attempting to draw attention to diminished water quality in area streams, "gimmicky" packaging might undermine the seriousness of your announcement and thus would not be appropriate. Instead, you would probably use a plain or specially designed folder or binding, or a similarly low-key website or CD-ROM, and include only straightforward, informational documents.

Decisions regarding whether to use a traditional or electronic format for your media kit require an honest assessment of your skills as well as a heavy dose of common sense. If you have scheduled a press conference, you should probably stick with a presentation folder with hard copies of relevant documents unless you have enough computers for every member of your audience. However, if you are communicating with members of the on-line media, if your media release announces some technological innovation (a new feature on your website, for example), or if your audience is geographically dispersed, then it would be more appropriate rhetorically as well as more efficient to use CD-ROMs or announce your news via an e-mail message that includes a link to your media kit. If you do not have the skills to construct electronic media kits even when the rhetorical situation recommends them, you may need to take a class or attend some workshops.

Public Information Kits and Action Kits

Media coverage is only one action in the public interest; there are many others. In response to various other situations in which rhetorical audiences need information before they can take action, media kits have expanded their focus into other kinds of kits.

Public information kits assemble information and resources that can be consulted by audiences as needed. Every year at the end of May, for example, Wilmington, North Carolina, sponsors a "Hurricane Expo," distributing free public information kits that include a hurricane tracking map, a map of evacuation routes and shelters, a checklist of preparation tips, and emergency phone numbers. The Expo takes place *before* the beginning of hurricane season so that people will have the information they need to prepare for an emergency. Not all public information kits respond to such potentially urgent situations, however. As a new student at your college or university, you probably received a folder filled with flyers, brochures, maps, and calendars related to campus services and events. Whether students actually consult this information (or remember they have it) is debatable, but the university does have an obligation to make the information as accessible as possible.

Action kits are issue-oriented, often politicized versions of public information kits. Individuals or groups—political candidates and advocacy organizations, for example—may create action kits for the use of supporters as they undertake local campaigns or activist projects. Most advocacy groups make action kits available for downloading on their websites; look for links labeled "Get Active," "Take Action," "Media Center," and the like. People for the Ethical Treatment of Animals (PETA) calls its action kits "Animal Angels Packs," and other groups have coined similarly creative names.

Although media kits, action kits, and public information kits differ in both audience and purpose, they contain many of the same attachments—mission statements, contact information, and FAQs among them. There are some differences, however. For example, while media kits almost always include a media release, public information kits almost never do; action kits, meanwhile, may include templates for media releases, appeal letters, or letters of concern for their audience to use or adapt for their own activist efforts. While media kits typically go through a gatekeeper, action kits and public information kits usually go directly to a rhetorical audience and are therefore constrained by fewer conventions regarding format, style, and delivery. As always, the content and presentation of an action kit or public information kit must be appropriate for its purpose and audience.

James and Chandler prepared a public information kit to distribute to students and staff at the back-to-school activities fair in an effort to generate interest in SCAT, the Yellow Bike program, and alternative transportation methods in general. Worried that presentation folders would appear too serious and that students might throw them away without even looking at the contents, James and Chandler persuaded SCAT to allocate money for the purchase of inexpensive water bottles printed with the SCAT logo. They then stuffed these bottles with information about their organization, including a calendar of events and contact person, a bike registration form, a coupon for a free bike tune-up, and a shuttle schedule. Clearly, James and Chandler were promoting specific actions among members of their audience. But their innovative public information campaign avoids the hard sell, instead giving students resources that will make it easy to take the propsed actions when they're ready.

Exercise

In your writer's notebook, make a list of organizations you belong to or are interested in joining; add to that list names of any individuals or groups you can think of who are involved in some interesting project (e.g., a political campaign, a dog walk-a-thon). Choose one individual or group from your list and schedule an appointment to talk to them about their interests, goals, and any upcoming events they will be involved in. Collect any written documents the person or group has designed for their own use or to promote their projects or concerns.

Once you've done this initial research, design a media kit, action kit, or public information kit for the individual or group: decide what attachments would inform a rhetorical audience and persuade them to act, what kind of presentation would be appropriate, and why. A campus group whose primary goals are social might have different needs than one whose purposes are more service-oriented; likewise, community groups might have different needs than student groups. If you feel committed to the person or group you profile, you might want to create the media, action, or public information kit for their use.

At the top of Tracy's list of organizations was the Community Action Group, a nonpartisan, interracial group that met regularly to discuss local concerns. After doing her content analysis of local newspapers (see Chapter 5), Tracy thought that it might be useful to organize study groups related to recurrent themes in the local African-American newspaper, the *Wilmington Journal*. Her goal was to create an alternative public sphere in which citizens might develop literacy skills along with political skills to be more active in their communities. When Tracy proposed her idea to the Community Action Group, members were supportive but cautious; they wanted more information. Tracy agreed to compile a sample action kit related to one of the central concerns in the Journal: fair housing.

After researching the issue, compiling materials, and taking pages of notes, Tracy realized that she was unsure what kind of action she wanted to promote: the study group itself or actions related to fair housing? After discussing her confusion with some classmates, she decided that she really needed to assemble two kinds of kits: an action kit to prepare people to participate in the study groups and a public information kit with resources related to each issue. Tracy assembled the following attachments for her action kit:

> photocopies of short articles on community literacy
>
> sample flyer to promote the study groups
>
> FAQs about the study group (e.g., Do I have to attend every meeting? How do I know what issues will be discussed?)

recommended meeting agenda (5 minutes for introductions, etc.)

tips on facilitating group discussions

name tags

notebook to record details of discussions: names of participants, key points of discussion, decisions made or actions taken

extensive list of on-line resources

Tracy's public information kit on fair housing included the following attachments:

recent news articles from the *Journal* and other publications

Tenant's Bill of Rights, Landlord's Bill of Rights

copies of relevant laws and ordinances (local, state, and federal)

Fair Housing Information Sheets (e.g., early termination of a lease, structural modifications for disabled residents of public and Section 8 housing, exemptions from "no pets" clauses, linguistic profiling)

consumer information: mortgages, loans, etc.

forms and tips for filing a housing discrimination complaint

list of local agencies that deal with housing issues

list of local public defenders who accept fair housing cases

information on how to organize a residents association

extensive list of on-line resources

If you were a member of Tracy's group—or the Community Action Group—how would you respond to her proposed kits? Can you anticipate other information that might be useful to include? What suggestions would you offer? How would you present the kits?

Peer Review

Before writing a media release or preparing a media, action, or public information kit, you should work through the "Thinking Rhetorically" checklists in Chapters 3 and 4 to make sure these are appropriate responses to an urgent rhetorical situation. Before submitting your documents to a suitable audience, ask someone you trust to read it with the following questions in mind:

- Is it clear why the rhetorical situation to which this document responds is urgent for a public audience?

- What action(s) does this document call for? Does the document give the audience enough information to take those actions easily and effectively?

- How would you characterize the language, tone, style, and presentation of the document(s)? Are these appropriate to the audience and purpose?

- Does the document conform to style and format conventions for media releases and media, action, or public information kits?

- In the case of media, action, or public information kits, do any documents strike you as irrelevant or inappropriate? If so, why?

- In the case of media, action, or public information kits, are there any gaps in information that could be addressed by additional attachments? If so, what are they?

- After reading the document(s), are you inclined to take the actions the writer proposes? Why or why not?

- If there are any problems, how might they be addressed in a revision?

Press Conferences

Press conferences provide opportunities for media interaction with your news in the form of photo opportunities, question and answer sessions, or other experiences. For example, at the end of a press conference announcing a coral reef research project, a group of scientists invited members of the media to scuba dive down to its undersea laboratory. Press conferences are usually accompanied by media kits and press releases and should be reserved for very significant announcements. If an organization calls press conferences too often, the media won't be able to distinguish the urgent news from the merely routine announcement and may stop paying attention.

The anatomy of a press conference works something like this:

1. Determine the importance of the news.
   - Is it urgent?
   - How can its urgency be conveyed to the media?

2. Set up the press conference.
   - How should the press conference be announced (e.g., by phone, fax, regular mail, or e-mail)?
   - Who should serve as the spokesperson?
   - What should we say?
   - What time and location are appropriate to the message?

3. Create appropriate documents. These may include:
   - Press release and/or media kits for members of the media

- • "Talking points" or remarks for spokesperson(s)
- • Agenda

4. Structure the press conference. Typical features include:
   - • Welcome to media and guests
   - • Description of the contents of the media kit, if any
   - • Introduction of the spokesperson
   - • Remarks
   - • Formal question and answer period
   - • Photo and interview opportunities (e.g., media outlets talk to speaker for sound bites)

As with media kits, gimmicks within press conferences are only appropriate to promote soft news. For example, when one municipal sports complex recently installed baby changing stations, it held a press conference in the men's bathroom—an announcement that probably had only minor significance for most people and was likely to be ignored by the media. However, by scheduling the press conference to correspond with a basketball game attended by many media representatives, the organizer was able to create news—in this case, efforts to create a family-friendly sports facility.

Although some press conferences might be lively and informal, nothing you do or say in that setting is "off the record." In other words, it's important to behave professionally at all times: anticipate logistical complications and stay in control. It goes without saying, furthermore, that spokespersons should speak clearly and dress appropriately for the event; usually this means conservative clothing.

Exercise

Call the public information office for your school or local government, and ask if there is an upcoming press conference you can attend. If possible, go to the press conference and in your writer's notebook, take notes on how the spokesperson(s) organize and orchestrate the event. What do they wear? How do they speak and behave? How do they handle logistical details such as scheduling, seating, late arrivals, noise, or interruptions? In your opinion, are the details of the press conference appropriate to the rhetorical situation?

CHAPTER 8

Focus on Grant Proposals

If you've ever applied for a scholarship or other money to help defray the costs of going to college, then you've applied for a grant. While these kinds of grants aren't exactly in the public interest (except in the sense that an educated citizenry is in the public interest), the application process is similar to the requests for financial support that are submitted by schools, nonprofit organizations, and other individuals and groups every day. Each of these groups is trying to persuade an audience to give them money for some worthy project.

Although grant money is widely available, grant proposals are among the most complicated genres of public writing, and competition for funding can be fierce. For these reasons, skilled grant writers are highly sought after by groups and institutions working in the public interest. Grants are usually awarded to organized institutions or nonprofit groups, many of which employ professional grant writers. Nevertheless, grant money is also accessible to everyday citizens who come together to solve problems. This chapter will discuss how to use writing to locate and take advantage of grant opportunities.

Finding the Right Funding Opportunities

National, local, global, and everyday public spheres offer a variety of grant opportunities. They range from the very large (millions of dollars, often to support extensive projects with several participants and disbursed over several years) to the very small (as little as $500 or less). The Ben & Jerry's Foundation, for example, offers grants to nonprofit groups throughout the United States for projects that meet the Foundation's criteria. Although it primarily offers "full grants" ($1001–$15,000), it also considers applications for "small grants" (up to $1000) "for innovative programs that fit into our general guidelines and that are infused with a spirit of hopefulness."

The Ben & Jerry's Foundation also distributes small grants to "Community Action Teams" within its home state of Vermont, and indeed, many granting institutions prefer to fund projects that have a direct and positive impact on a local—that is, geographically specific—public sphere. Families, civic groups, and local businesses often establish

Special Activity Fund Guidelines

The purpose of the Special Activity Fund is to support educational and student centered programs and activities. Priority is given to projects and events that are open to the entire campus community. Further priority is given to organizations that have attempted their own fundraising. Any person or group requesting funds must be prepared to demonstrate how the UNCW campus will benefit from the project.

Organizations must complete the following two steps in order to request funds:

1. Schedule a Time to Present your Request to the Appropriations Committee.
In order to request Special Activity Funds, student organizations must schedule a time to present their request to the Appropriations Committee. Presentations generally take ten to fifteen minutes and give the committee a comprehensive breakdown of the total project including the anticipated cost along with the purpose and scope of the event. **Please type all additional material and bring enough copies for 15 committee members.**

2. Prepare for your Appropriations Committee Presentation
Please complete the following application and return it to the SGA Treasurer by the Monday preceding your presentation. Include all information and documentation that pertains to the funding request including your current budget (including expenses and revenue), conference or event paperwork, order forms, or registration materials.

> **For best consideration by the Appropriations Committee, please submit all requests at least three weeks prior to the event or project date. Please note, all Appropriation Committee recommendations must go before the SGA Senate for approval. Special Activity Fund Requests are not final until the SGA Senate makes a formal vote.**

Funding Guidelines

Travel	Equipment	Programming
• SGA will only fund up to four (4) people going on a trip	• All organizations must log their equipment with the SGA Business Manager annually	• Priority is given to events that are open to the entire campus community
• SGA will fund up to $85 per person for registration	• The president is responsible for the upkeep and care of the equipment	• Organizations must print "funded by the SGA" on all promotional materials for the event
• SGA will fund up to $43 per person per night	• Negligence will result in confiscation of equipment	• A list of all co-sponsors must accompany the Special Activity Fund request to the Appropriations Committee
• SGA will fund $0.23/mile up to 400 miles	• All property is state property (must adhere to university guidelines)	
• Food will not be covered		

Figure 8.1a. The Student Government Association at the University of North Carolina at Wilmington offers grants to support student-initiated projects and events through its Special Activity Fund. It is limited to, and designed to benefit, members of a geographically specific public sphere and thus represents an example of local public literacy.

charitable foundations to benefit the residents of their community. The Cooper Foundation in Waco, Texas, for example, describes its mission as "mak[ing] Waco a better or more desirable city in which to live." In order to address this very local goal, the Foundation offers grants "exclusively to nonprofit organizations in the Waco area."

Special Activity Fund Request

_____
(Date Submitted)

_____
(Name of Organization)   (Number of Members)

_____
(Contact Person)   (Phone)

_____
(Date of Presentation)   (Time of Presentation)

Request for: ☐ Travel   ☐ Equipment   ☐ Programming   ☐ Other

Please Describe the Purpose of the Request: _____
_____
_____
_____
_____
_____
_____
_____
_____
_____
_____
_____
_____

Please List Any Co-Sponsors: _____
_____
_____

Please List the Anticipated Revenue: _____
_____
_____

Total Cost: _____

**All Special Activity request must be accompanied by supporting documentation
in order to be considered by the Appropriations Committee.
Please see the reverse side of this form for details to be provided.
Please type all additional materials and bring fifteen copies of each
to your presentation.**

Figure 8.1b.

Because they generally exist "off the radar," everyday grant opportunities are probably the most difficult to find. They are available informally through private donors or unincorporated groups (e.g., neighborhood associations) rather than through nonprofit agencies and philanthropic institutions. Everyday grants generally aren't advertised; in fact, individuals or groups who are willing to fund projects in the public interest might not even plan to do so until they are approached with a promising idea. If this is one of the constraints you are facing as you apply for a grant, you might need to work harder to demonstrate the urgency of the problem you are addressing and the feasibility of the solution you are proposing.

Supporting Documentation

Please provide the following information, typed, on a separate sheet of paper:
(see inside for guidelines)

For Travel Requests:

1. Destination
2. Lodging arrangements / Cost
3. Transportation / Cost
4. Registration / Cost
5. Number of people traveling
6. Amount fundraised by group
7. Total cost of travel
8. Total amount requested

For Programming Requests:

1. Date of event
2. Location
3. Cost of Admission (if charging)
4. Amount fundraised by group
5. Total cost of program
6. Total amount requested

For Equipment Requests:

1. Cost of equipment
2. Vendor
3. Include at least two other estimates for goods
4. Amount fundraised by group
5. Storage / Maintenance Plan
6. Total cost of equipment
7. Total amount requested

For All Other Requests:

1. Present a detailed account of request
2. Include estimates
3. Total amount of item or project
4. Total amount requested

**Please remember to contact the SGA Treasurer
to schedule a presentation for your organization to
the Appropriations Committee
962-3553.**

Figure 8.1c.

Some varieties of everyday grant support are even more informal. If you ask your parents to help pay your college expenses, for example, you might agree to certain conditions and even put the terms of the support (e.g., maintaining a minimum GPA) into a written contract. Such requests can also be made in the public interest. For example, you might write a note to your landlord asking him to waive the normal rental fee for your apartment complex's conference facilities so that a service organization that you belong to can hold meetings there.

Grant opportunities are frequently announced in newspapers and newsletters, and on flyers and websites, through "requests for proposals," or *RFPs.* At the library, you can find directories of such opportunities through the subject headings *grants-in-aid, block grants, fundraising,* and *charitable contributions.* On-line, you have several options. One technique is to conduct a search for grant directories on Yahoo! or some other search engine using such terms as *grants, block grants, small grants, grant opportunities,* or *charitable foundations.* This type of search will connect you with some of the hundreds of directories of granting agencies as well as to individual funders. A more efficient technique is to do a keyword search that begins with the words *small grants—small grants community gardens,* for example, or *small grants music festivals.* You may need to experiment with several keywords and several search engines before you find the information you want.

If you are interested in a specific issue, such as AIDS or disability rights, you can consult advocacy magazines that share your concerns, such as *POZ* or *The Able Informer,* or visit websites that deal with these issues. Many of these websites regularly post RFPs and may even send you an e-mail message alerting you to new funding opportunities.

It usually doesn't take long before you find yourself on the trail of dozens of promising funders and funding opportunities, and once you start communicating with a few of these groups you may find yourself with more opportunities than you have time to pursue. If you can't find anything, though, most universities also have research offices which match faculty and students with appropriate funding sources, assist them in applying for grants, and sponsor grant-writing workshops.

Like other genres of public writing, grants respond to urgent rhetorical situations: problems that have potential solutions but no money to implement them. Such situations are perhaps most frequently encountered by nonprofit organizations, which derive their resources from donations, grants, and bequests and thus work with limited and often unpredictable budgets.

When writing an appeal letter (see Chapter 6), your rhetorical audience is composed of individual *donors.* When writing a grant proposal, your rhetorical audience consists primarily of *funders,* or granting institutions, that might be willing to provide financial support for your project. Of course, institutions are composed of individuals. Therefore, as with many other public genres, grant proposals go first to gatekeepers—in this case, reviewers who screen all grant proposals and decide which ones are in the public interest. "Public interest" is defined differently by different institutions, so when you are considering possible grant opportunities, look for compatibility between the purpose and goals of your project and those of the granting institution. Although you will likely find several RFPs that seem well suited to your project, you might have to adapt your project description to meet grant criteria.

Exercise

Look through your writer's notebook for recurring interests, themes, or problems. Then, using the search strategies described above, locate several granting sources and RFPs that might be appropriate for supporting projects related to those issues. (For example, if you are very concerned about domestic violence, then look for RFPs that share this concern.) If you find the RFP in a book or periodical, write a letter requesting an application packet; if you find it on-line, print out application materials and organize them in a folder.

Don't worry about responding to a specific rhetorical situation just yet. It's enough at this point to familiarize yourself with the process of locating grant opportunities and making sense of their sometimes-convoluted guidelines. If you already have an idea for a project that merits funding—or if an RFP inspires some good ideas—record them in your writer's notebook and narrow your search.

Applying for a Grant: Three Steps

I. Preparation

Before you even start looking for a grant, you should do some preliminary writing to define your project's *goals* (what you want to accomplish) and *objectives* (how you will accomplish them). For example, SCAT's central goal was to expand transportation alternatives on campus and in their local community, and their initial objectives were to obtain and refurbish bikes for the Yellow Bike program (see Chapter 4). It's also a good idea at this stage to identify who will benefit from your project (both directly and indirectly) and how you will evaluate its success or progress.

Once you've outlined the basic purposes of your project, you can search for funders who share your priorities. Your first step after locating potential grant opportunities is to contact the funders and acquire applications and proposal guidelines, which include information about eligibility, submission deadlines, format requirements, and the proposal evaluation process. If possible, obtain a list of projects that the granting institution has supported in the past; this can give you an idea of whether your proposal has a good chance of being successful. This information is usually available on-line.

Grant guidelines and applications offer many clues as to what granting institutions value: current program interests, funding priorities, evaluation criteria, and so on. This information should suggest intellectual themes for your proposal and may even provide a vocabulary for articulating exactly how your proposal matches the interests of the funder. Although it is often possible to propose the same project to several funders, submission policies and evaluation criteria vary widely even among grants with similar priorities. Be prepared to modify your proposal to meet the requirements of each grant.

National and local granting institutions generally do not award grants to individuals working independently in the public interest. Instead, they prefer to support projects undertaken by organized groups with an established identity, mission, and track record. Some applications may limit funding to nonprofit agencies, in which case applicants may have to provide documentation for their "501(c)(3) status" (see Chapter 4), including financial reports, a list of members of the Board of Directors, and so on.

2. Writing the Proposal

Most funders offer detailed guidelines on how to apply for grants. You should read these carefully for specifications regarding content, length, format, and other requirements. Ben & Jerry's, for example, states that application letters and proposals "should employ a readable font size (no less than 10 pt.) and one inch margins." The Bright Ideas educational grant, sponsored by the North Carolina Electric Membership Corporation, emphasizes that "Faxed applications will NOT be accepted."

It's not uncommon for you to run across RFPs that simply ask you to "submit a proposal." Luckily, grant proposals include several standard features that you can use and adapt even if the granting agency doesn't provide more thorough guidelines. These features include the following:

Statement of need: purpose and goals of project, measurable objectives, and compelling reasons why the proposal should be supported; background on the problem your project is designed to improve

- Use a funnel approach: start with the generalized problem as it occurs in your community and move to the conditions which make this a problem.
- Describe current resources that address the problem, identify gaps in those resources, and explain how your proposal will fill these gaps.
- Prepare to do whatever research is necessary to offer evidence of the need for the program and the appropriateness and feasibility of your solution.

Plan: method and process of accomplishing goals and objectives

- Specify actions or measures you will take to achieve your goals.
- Describe personnel qualifications (including volunteers).
- Tailor the description of the project to the interests, priorities, and goals of the funding source.

Evaluation: how you will know whether you are meeting your goals

- Describe plans for record keeping and assessment of data.
- Identify measurable milestones that you will reach along the way.

Project timeline: start and finish dates; schedule of activities

Credentials: information about the applicant and organization that verifies your ability to successfully undertake project, including history and mission of organization, population served, and previous accomplishments

Budget: cost projections

- Don't round out numbers; use bids and estimates when possible.
- Don't pad: if reviewers suspect that you are deceiving them on budget projections, they might question other parts of your application.
- Include all sources of support, including donations, volunteer time, and so on.

Supporting materials: additional information requested as part of your application (e.g., letters of reference, resumes)

Proposals are typically written in narrative form, with the categories listed above (or other categories specified by the guidelines) functioning as subheadings to enhance the readability of your document. You should double space between paragraphs and subsections of the narrative, and you may wish to format your proposal in block style. (This textbook makes use of both of these formatting conventions; see also Chapter 6.) The content and form of a grant can be adapted to meet the needs of different rhetorical situations—for example, proposing a project at school or at your workplace for which you need guidance or time off, but no money.

The easiest thing to remember when applying for a grant is also one of the most important: *follow instructions*. Most grant reviewers appreciate concise proposals that they can read and understand quickly. So if the guidelines request a one-page letter, don't send a two-page letter. If the application requires you to enclose several items with your proposal, make yourself a checklist (if there isn't one in your application packet) and include all of them. If there is a submission deadline, mark it on your calendar and allow yourself plenty of time to meet it (including time to get necessary signatures and mail your materials). Failure to follow directions won't necessarily mean that your proposal will be rejected or ignored, but why take chances?

3. Follow-Up

Funding organizations usually inform applicants once they have received your materials. If you don't hear from them, it's appropriate to contact them about the status of your proposal.

Eventually you will be notified whether or not the funder has chosen to support your project. If your proposal was unsuccessful, don't give up. Most grant reviewers are willing to provide feedback about a proposal's strengths and weaknesses, and this information can help you to revise your proposal for resubmission. Agencies that receive a large volume of submissions might not be available to provide extensive feedback, in which case you might want to consult a more experienced grant writer for guidance. The research office at your university might provide this service at no charge.

If your proposal was successful, write a thank you letter to the funder immediately. If you are expected to submit written reports or other materials documenting your project's progress or success, take these responsibilities seriously. Since many grants are renewable, you must do all you can to assure funders that they made the right decision in supporting your project.

Regardless of whether your project receives support, it's important to maintain productive, professional relationships with granting agencies. This is especially true in local and everyday public spheres, where funders may also be neighbors or peers—and where the beneficiaries of your project are likely not only to know you personally but to depend on you to work in their interest. Money introduces a variety of constraints into the rhetorical situation, which public writers must anticipate and appropriately address.

Peer Review

As always, you should work through the "Thinking Rhetorically" checklists in Chapters 3 and 4 before undertaking a grant proposal. Prior to submitting your proposal to a funder, provide a copy of the submission guidelines to someone you trust and ask that person to read both the guidelines and your proposal carefully with these questions in mind:

- What is the purpose of this proposal? Does it clearly and concisely identify the problem and explain why the writer finds this situation urgent? Does it propose a specific, feasible, measurable action?

- Is the proposal addressed to an appropriate rhetorical audience? Does it meet the eligibility criteria of the grant (if any)? Is the proposed project consistent with the interests of the funding source?

- Does the application and/or proposal include all required information and materials?

- Does it echo the language and intellectual themes of the grant? Does it clearly align the project with the interests, goals, and priorities of the funding source?

- Does it conform to the style, format, and length specifications (if any) described in the grant guidelines? Does it employ features that enhance readability?

- How would you characterize the language, tone, and style of the application/proposal? Are these appropriate to the document's audience and purpose?

- After reading the application/proposal, are you persuaded that this project deserves funding? Why or why not?

- Is there anything in the application or proposal that would benefit from additional research? If so, what?

- If there are any problems, how might they be addressed in a revision?

Grant Writing in Action

Kimberle and Summer's writing and conversations (see Chapters 3 and 4) revealed a mutual interest in women's health care and a mutual concern about the costs of such care at their campus Wellness Center—costs which prevented many female students from obtaining essential services. After discussing a variety of possible responses to this rhetorical situation, Kimberle and Summer decided to write a grant proposal requesting money to establish a fund to cover these costs for students who could not otherwise afford them. Since most funders do not work with individuals working in the public interest, Kimberle and Summer established a group called FACT of Life and applied for 501(c)(3) status. While their application materials were being processed, they brainstormed the following lists of goals and objectives:

Project Goals

make students aware that their health fee does not necessarily cover their services

encourage women to get annual pap smears

make students (esp. women) aware of the connection between Well Woman exams and the early detection of breast and cervical cancers—also, women as young as 18 are at risk for these cancers!

educate Wellness Center staff about the importance of these exams and why additional charges make it impossible for some students to afford them

get money to cover these tests into permanent university budget (eventually)

Objectives

decide who is eligible for funding—everyone? must students demonstrate need?

figure out how to disburse money—directly to Wellness Center? through student's account?

evaluation of program—whether it's being used, etc.

education

publicity campaign

coordinate information and procedures with Wellness Center and Women's Resource Center

As they reviewed their lists, Kimberle and Summer arrived at several conclusions: first, their goals were more disparate than they realized; second, some goals sounded more like objectives and vice versa; and finally, there was not always a clear correlation between their goals and their objectives. They needed to prioritize, even if that meant focusing on only one goal. They decided, then, to focus on establishing what they called the "FACT of Life Fund," postponing for the time being the educational campaign and the protest over the misleading health care fee. If they were successful meeting that goal, they reasoned, they might be able to pursue a more ambitious agenda in the future.

Once they had articulated their basic goals and objectives, Summer and Kimberle's next step was to identify suitable funding opportunities, so they searched the Internet using the phrase *women's health grants*. However, they quickly discovered that such grants were either too big for their modest project (hundreds of thousands of dollars or more, designed to support research or implement large-scale institutional changes) or limited to professional health care providers. Using the phrase *small grants women's health*, Kimberle and Summer located several RFPs, but even these seemed to target established groups who could demonstrate a successful track record.

Frustrated, Kimberle and Summer visited their university's Office of Research Administration, where a counselor discussed their project with them and then showed them how to search the office's databases of funding opportunities. They eventually discovered the Landfall Foundation, a local funder which supports projects "targeted to health and welfare activities, education, and the arts [with] priority to organizations with low administrative overhead and high volunteer participation." After carefully studying the Foundation's guidelines, Summer and Kimberle reviewed the list of agencies which had been awarded grants during the previous funding cycle. Drawing as many inferences as possible from this sparse information, they made detailed notes regarding the Foundation's funding priorities, submission requirements, evaluation criteria, and intellectual themes. The scope of the grant program—$3000 or less—further assisted them in clarifying and prioritizing their goals.

The Landfall Foundation makes available the following application form:

LANDFALL FOUNDATION
2002 Funding Cycle

GRANT APPLICATION INFORMATION & FORMS

The Landfall Foundation is a charitable foundation formed in 1996 to establish a community support effort specifically originating from the residents of Landfall.

The Foundation seeks to allocate funds among HEALTH and WELFARE activities, EDUCATION, and the ARTS primarily in New Hanover County and contiguous counties of Brunswick and Pender.

As a matter of Foundation policy, we will not support political parties or candidates, organizations representing religious or denominational causes or associations or groups proven to have high administration or fund raising costs (20% or more). In addition, we encourage the use of volunteers to carry out the project's function and will likely not fund a project which depends on highly paid management, employees or contractors to reach its goals.

As the Landfall Foundation is a relatively new and small foundation, typical grants are distributed in the $500 to $3000 range. Landfall Foundation will give priority to projects where such amounts can make a difference. When the request to Landfall Foundation is part of a larger project, the request should identify a specific program within the larger project where Landfall Foundation's contributions can have a meaningful impact. Organizations that have been funded for three previous consecutive calendar years by the Landfall Foundation will not be considered in the 2002 cycle, and the Foundation will only consider one grant application per agency.

The Foundation awards grants once a year in the fall. Grant proposals must be received by 5 p.m. Friday, July 12, 2002 to be considered during the current grant review period. The following pages are provided to be used to request a grant from the Foundation. Please complete the forms and return four copies to:

The Landfall Foundation
1838 Gleneagles Lane
Wilmington, NC 28405

No material will be returned. Your application will be received and given first review by the screening committee. Upon acceptance by the screening committee, your application will then be submitted to the Foundation Board for final consideration and possible funding. Funding decisions will be made by November 1, 2002. All applicants will be notified about funding decisions, and checks should be received by Thanksgiving.

Figure 8.2a. Application and proposal guidelines, such as these provided by the Landfall Foundation, provide information about what a granting agency values.[1]

LANDFALL FOUNDATION
GRANT APPLICATION FORM

NAME OF PROJECT: _____

CATEGORY OF ENTRY: HEALTH & WELFARE_____ ART____EDUCATION_____

AMOUNT REQUESTED: _____

PART I: YOUR ORGANIZATION

Name:
_____

Street Address: _____

City, State, & Zip Code: _____

Name of Key Contact Person: _____

Title: _____ _____

e-mail address: _____

Organization Website: _____

Telephone # _____ Fax # _____

  1. Please attach a copy of your Federal Tax ID # and your 501 (C) (3) IRS tax-exemption
     letter with your application.

  2. Is your organization a private, non-operating foundation? If YES, you do not qualify for a
     grant. YES ( ) NO ( )

  3. Would a grant from the Landfall Foundation in the amount being requested jeopardize your
     tax-exempt status? YES ( ) NO ( )

  4. Will any of these funds be used to pay a nationally affiliated organization? If YES, please
     explain. YES ( ) NO ( )

  5. Does your organization now, or does it plan in the future, to engage in any way in the
     promotion or advancement of political causes or religious beliefs? If YES, please explain.
     YES ( ) NO ( )

  6. Briefly summarize your organization's background, goals, and current programs and how
     this grant would help your organization meet its goals.

  7. Describe your organization's structure and attach a list of your officers and directors.

Figure 8.2b.

Once they had located a funding opportunity, Summer and Kimberle reassessed the
rhetorical situation, recording in their writer's notebooks questions, resources, and potential constraints related to their project—issues they would have to reconsider or research further before addressing them in their grant application. These issues included:

> How do we show a connection between annual Well Woman check-ups and early
>   detection of cancer? NEED STATISTICS!!
>
> Should all female students be eligible or must they demonstrate financial need?
>
> What if 501(c)(3) confirmation doesn't arrive in time to apply for grant?

PART II: PROJECT/PROGRAM (Please quantify whenever possible.)

1. Briefly summarize your project (50 words or less).

2. Describe the need or opportunity that the proposed project will address.

3. Describe the objective of the project and indicate how individual lives of the recipients will be improved and how many people will benefit.

4. If this project is part of a larger program, describe how a Landfall Foundation grant will make a difference within the overall project and contribute significantly enough to receive individual recognition.

5. What strategies will you employ to accomplish the project objective?

6. State how, when, and who will conduct an evaluation to measure how well your project is meeting its objectives.

PART III: FINANCIAL INFORMATION

1. Amount requested from the Landfall Foundation---not to exceed $3000.

2. Develop a complete project budget, including income and expenses, to accomplish the project for which you are requesting funds.

3. List the names of organizations both public and private, to which you have applied for support for this specific project/program. Also show the amount requested and the status (pending, approved, or disapproved).

4. If the funds are to be used for construction or equipment acquisition, explain the bidding process.

PART IV: REPORTING REQUIREMENTS

Grantees are required to furnish a project progress report to the Landfall Foundation, 1924 Pembroke Jones Drive, Wilmington, NC 28405 by July 11, 2003.

Figure 8.2c.

What if we get the grant? Who will administer program once we graduate?

So far we only have anecdotal evidence that the costs of these tests is a problem for students—see if there is any data on how many students use the Wellness Center, get Well Woman exams, choose not to get WW exams because of extra costs, etc.

Since objectives require cooperation of Wellness Center to do this, do we need their permission to apply for this grant?

resources: cancer websites, hospital library, Women's Resource Center, Wellness Center (?), Office of Research Administration

After doing additional research, Kimberle and Summer had little trouble filling out Parts I and III of the application form. Part II, however, posed a number of problems. To begin with, they were unsure whether their proposed project addressed the need for *women's health services* or the need for *a fund to pay for these services* (Part II, question 2). Since their research demonstrated a clear causal relationship between Well Woman exams and the early detection of cervical, breast, and ovarian cancers, they decided to focus on the need for services. Thus they defined their objective (question 3) as "provid[ing] essential health services to female students who cannot afford the addition cost."

By the time they got to question 4, however, Kimberle and Summer were beginning to rethink their decision: they were not qualified to offer gynecological services and besides, the services were already available to students; the problem was that many students could not afford them or were unaware that they needed them. This realization caused Kimberle and Summer to revise their answer to questions 2 and 3 as follows:

Question 2: Describe the need or opportunity that the proposed project will address.

Original: Health care professionals consider it mandatory for every woman 18 years and older to receive an annual gynecological check-up, which includes a pelvic exam, Pap smear, and breast exam. No woman, no matter how young, is exempt from the possibility of developing cervical, ovarian, or breast cancer within her lifetime. Because early detection is key to curing these cancers, the Foundation's support would provide a meaningful impact toward saving young women's lives.

Revised: Costs for essential medical care for female college students are not covered by their mandatory student health fees, and many students cannot afford to pay the additional costs.

Question 3: Describe the objective [i.e., goal] of the project and indicate how individual lives of the recipients will be improved and how many people will benefit.

Original: It is our objective to provide essential life saving gynecological, or "Well Woman" exams to all female UNCW students, regardless of their ability to pay.

Revised: The goal of the FACT of Life Fund is to provide financial assistance to female students who cannot afford the additional $51 cost of essential gynecological services. This will improve the lives of at least 57 students by either saving their lives through early detection of cancer or providing peace of mind in knowing that they are cancer free.

[Statistics showing causal connection between regular gynecological exams and early detection of cancer; results of university-sponsored survey assessing student use of Wellness Center, awareness of fee structure, and most frequently requested services]

What follows is the fourth draft of Kimberle and Summer's responses to Part II of the Landfall Foundation grant application. Consult the criteria for effective grant writing, the materials provided by the Landfall Foundation, and the peer review questions listed earlier in this chapter. Then reread Summer and Kimberle's draft carefully. What suggestions would you offer them as they undertake their revisions?

Exercise

Alone or in small groups, brainstorm a list of problems on campus. Choose one problem, then brainstorm another list—this time, of projects that could improve or solve that problem. Then, using the guidelines for the SGA Special Activity Fund or a funding source at your own campus, write a one-paragraph description of the goals and objectives of your idea. Remember, grant reviewers appreciate writing that not only describes a project in clear, concise terms but also explains how the project fits the specific interests and priorities of the funding institution.

Note

1. *Seafunders.org.* July 2002. Southeast Public Interest Network of North Carolina, Inc. <http://www.seafunders.org/fundhead.htm>.

CHAPTER 9

Focus on Petitions and Ballot Initiatives

Much of the writing done in the public interest seems almost to appear out of thin air. City charters, municipal codes and regulations, organizational mission statements, forms, signs—these documents represent a ubiquitous part of the public literacy landscape, but where did they come from? The answer, of course, is that someone—or more likely, several people—wrote them. Since the rhetorical situations served by civic documents vary so widely, people with writing skills and a commitment to the public interest are needed at all levels of government. And yet, in order for a democracy to live up to its ideals, people outside the government must also take advantage of opportunities to participate in civic writing projects.

This chapter will discuss civic documents that are accessible to ordinary citizens and elected officials alike: petitions and ballot initiatives. A petition is a formal written request for action which demonstrates support for that request through signatures of affected individuals. Petitions can be used in national, local, global, and everyday public spheres and thus hold potential for broad and meaningful influence on everything from legislation to television shows to the color of M&M's. There are two basic kinds of petition: those that are legally binding and those that are not. Legally binding petitions are the first step toward enacting ballot initiatives, which are legislative proposals recommended by citizens for popular vote.

Non-Binding Petitions

A *non-binding petition* is basically a letter of concern (see Chapter 6) signed by many people and forwarded to a rhetorical audience in hopes of influencing some action. Usually this audience is a government official who might be persuaded to vote for or against a proposed bill. Sometimes, though, petitions are sent to industry leaders, presidents of corporations, and other powerful individuals as a means of expressing an opinion about a product, service, or policy.

Advocacy organizations like Viewers for Quality Television are vigilant about identifying rhetorical situations likely to be considered urgent by their members and may coordinate petition drives: saving a show threatened by cancellation, for example, or pressuring the networks to keep sexually explicit material out of prime time. It is becoming increasingly common to conduct these campaigns electronically, through e-mail alerts and downloadable texts. Dozens of Internet sites "host" petitions free of charge and some even provide a template to help writers generate these documents.

Because non-binding petitions carry no legal force, their conventions regarding content and form are fairly flexible, even in national and global public spheres. Your best bet is to write an open letter or letter of concern (see Chapter 6) and solicit the signatures of people you know personally. Don't worry if you only have a few supporters: while on-line petition campaigns can reach many more potential allies (and while electronic signatures themselves are legally binding), they can also backfire—and badly. A few years ago, an on-line petition to stop the Taliban's torture and domestic incarceration of women in Afghanistan circulated so widely that the flood of responses overwhelmed the electronic mailboxes designed to collect them. Other on-line petitions have been forwarded so many times that they never reach their destinations.[1]

Although it can be discouraging to learn that a petition may have no effect, the fact is that even very popular petitions may not serve the public interest. Let's say, for example, that a test for one of your classes was scheduled for the last day of the final exam period, preventing you and your classmates from leaving for your end-of-semester break in a timely fashion. In response to this rhetorical situation, you create an everyday petition that describes the problem and says, "We the undersigned respectfully request that the final exam for this class be rescheduled to the first day of the exam period." Would your professor be obligated to take this action simply because the request was supported by a majority of students? Clearly, the answer is no. Just because an action is popular doesn't mean that it is feasible, beneficial, or legal, and no rhetorical audience should comply with a request from an organized group of people simply because they appear to represent the majority.

Some rhetorical audiences believe that non-binding petitions occupy the bottom of the civic action feeding chain. In other words, because they cannot be legally enforced, they represent the least effective means to bring about changes. As a writer you should be aware of and take seriously this constraint, but you need not give up completely. Non-binding petitions do have the potential to persuade rhetorical audiences to take desired actions. And at a time when money can unduly influence the political process, they preserve the American tradition of direct democratic participation and thus represent an important genre even if used for informal rhetorical situations.

Exercise

There are dozens of on-line petition hosting sites, including *http://www.the-petitionsite.com*, *http://www.petitions.org*, and *http://www.petitionpetition.com*. You can find others by typing *petitions* into a search engine like Google. Alone or in small groups, explore one or more of these sites and look carefully at the petitions posted there, noting such rhetorical features as tone, audience, and format. In general, what kinds of issues and rhetorical situations do these petitions address? Are these issues in the public interest? Which petitions, if any, do you find most credible, and why?

Some on-line petitions include "comments" sections that allow people to explain why they support a proposed action. If possible, locate and read some of these comments. What do they reveal about why people sign non-binding petitions? What do they reveal about the purposes of on-line petitions and hosting sites?

Legally Binding Petitions

Legally binding petitions might be compared to "basic research" in the natural and social sciences: they establish foundations from which to launch more complex and challenging projects. In many cases, they play an integral role in the legislative process. Unlike non-binding petitions, legally binding petitions are addressed to a rhetorical audience of individuals, usually voters, whose signatures indicate their support for a proposed action.

While conventions for all public genres are shaped by rhetorical situations, this is especially true of civic documents like legally binding petitions, which are subject to a variety of rules and procedures established by the government in order to guarantee consistency and fairness. Before initiating a legally binding petition, it's imperative that you research these requirements; this information can easily be found by visiting the appropriate government offices (e.g., Board of Elections), either in person or on-line. Your research should provide answers to the following questions:

- What city, county, or state office(s) approve(s) petitions? What resources, if any, do they offer citizens to assist them in designing these documents?

- What requirements regarding content and form, if any, must writers comply with in order for their petitions to be considered legally binding?

- How many signatures are needed to "qualify" a petition? What constitutes a valid signature?

- What is the approval or qualifying process for petitions? What are the deadlines, if any, for each stage of this process?

The petition process can be complex and confusing, so it's important to stay organized. Make yourself a checklist, put all deadlines on your calendar and allow yourself plenty of time to meet them, maintain a careful record of your progress, and write down names and contact information for anyone who can help you to achieve your efforts.

Once you fully understand the legislative processes in which you want your petition to participate, you must translate rules and procedures into genre conventions. Certain kinds of information are required in order for the signatures—and thus the petitions themselves—to be considered valid. These requirements are meant to give petitions credibility, which is important not only for government officials but also for potential supporters. Petitions can be formatted horizontally or vertically on the page, and most include the following features:

Descriptive Title: typed in all capital letters and centered at the top of the page

Summary: describes the problem and proposed action in clear, succinct language; single-spaced under title

Spaces for Names, Addresses, Signatures, and Voter Status: categories are determined by local or state rules; arranged in column format

Sponsor(s): name(s) and contact information for person(s) or group(s) sponsoring the petition drive and responsible for answering questions about the petitions and submitting them to the appropriate agency

Other: any other information (mandatory or optional) that would assist in qualifying the petition, educating voters, or encouraging commitment to the issue to which the petition responds

All of this information must appear on every page of your petition. It is not acceptable, for example, to write the title and summary of your proposal on a separate sheet of paper and attach several pages of signatures. For this reason, your petition should never be more than one page long.

Of course, the most important part of any petition is the description of the problem and proposed change. Before you design your petition, you should think carefully about what you would like to accomplish: your actions must be feasible, legal, beneficial to many members of the public, and enforceable. The degree of detail you use depends on a number of factors, including your budget, the complexity of the issue, and local requirements regulating the form and content of petitions. As with other requests for action (e.g., letters of concern), all information printed on your petition must be completely accurate, as signatures obtained through the use of fraudulent, misleading, or erroneous information will automatically be invalidated. Furthermore, it is best to avoid extreme emotional appeals, even with very controversial issues.

Many petitions must gather a minimum number of signatures before they can move forward through the legislative process. This number varies not only from place to place but from year to year. In order to qualify a state ballot initiative, the number may be as little as 1% or as much as 20% of voters in the most recent election. For more informal petitions, you might only need to demonstrate "widespread" support.

Everyone who signs a petition must prove that they are authorized to do so. Usually this means that they must be registered voters in the affected area–the state of Colorado, for example. In other instances, however, their voting status is irrelevant, and they might only have to show that they live in the neighborhood or attend the university where the proposed action will occur. For this reason, your petition should always include spaces for names and addresses as well as signatures. Although post office boxes or dorm room numbers might be acceptable for petitions circulated on a college campus, state and local governments require street addresses. Most petitions undergo an exacting validation process during which this information is authenticated; always make photocopies of your petition in case questions arise during this process.

Page ___ of ___

NEIGHBORHOOD TRAFFIC STUDY PETITION

If your neighborhood has appropriate traffic calming devices implemented, average traffic speeds may be reduced by 3 to 8 mph and traffic volumes may be reduced by 0 to 10%. However, some devices are known to increase noise (hitting speed bumps, acceleration, braking) and require pavement markings and signs. ***Most importantly, some traffic calming devices are permanent fixtures.***

The undersigned hereby petition the City of Wilmington for **traffic calming measures** on ____________________ between ____________________ and ____________________.

Name *One per household*	Address	Signature	Telephone	OK to install bump or other traffic calming device in front of my home. *Please Initial*

The contact person is:____________________ Address:____________________ Phone:____________________

Return all petition forms to: City of Wilmington, Traffic Engineering, Attn: William McDow, PO Box 1810, Wilmington, NC 28402

Please make a copy of this petition for your records.

Figure 9.1. This local petition features a brief summary of the issue under consideration and allows for up to 13 signatures on each page. In order for the proposed action to occur, 51% of the residents of the affected neighborhood must sign the petition.

As the process of writing and circulating petitions illustrates, knowing how to write civic documents is valuable only when you also understand how government works. It's part of our ongoing education as citizens and as public writers to learn not just the rudiments of the legislative, executive, and judicial branches but also the nitty-gritty of what constitutes a valid signature on a petition and when it's illegal for elected officials to meet behind closed doors. Although this knowledge can be cumbersome, it serves the public interest by maintaining the integrity of the legislative process.

Ballot Initiatives

Once your petition has been approved, your next step may be to pursue a *ballot initiative*. Ballot initiatives usually address very controversial isues, such as whether a state should establish a lottery, reinstate the death penalty, or set aside money for green space. Most city and county charters include provisions by which citizens can propose legislation through ballot initiatives, but currently only 24 state consitutions do. Residents of those other 26 states must depend on politicians to enact legislation in the public interest through *ballot referenda*, proposals "referred" by elected officials.[2]

Before an initiative qualifies for the ballot, its supporters must circulate a petition among registered voters and obtain the number of signatures mandated by the state constitution or city charter. Arizona, for example, requires the signatures of 10% of the number of votes cast in the last gubernatorial election; other states require a percentage of signatures from each legislative district. At the end of the canvassing process, signatures are counted and validated to determine whether the initiative has "qualified" to appear on the ballot. Since some signatures may be disqualified (e.g., because a person signed the petition twice), it is wise to collect more than the minimum number required.

The procedures for submitting ballot initiatives are complex and vary widely, which is why you should consult relevant government resources before embarking on this process. The following websites can help point you in the right direction:

> *The Civic Mind:* gateway site that provides information on "hot" public issues, current citizen initiatives (including educational programs), and civic renewal
>
> > http://www.civicmind.com/ballot.htm
>
> *The Ballot Initiative Strategy Center:* offers resources and support for citizens launching campaigns, as well as comprehensive and up-to-date information on job opportunities, election reform, voter education, and the status of current state initiatives
>
> > http://www.ballot.org

As with petitions, the genre conventions for ballot initiatives derive primarily from procedural requirements and thus vary according to specific contexts and locations. Most include the following features:

> *Statute Number:* assigned by a government agency after petitions are approved
>
> *Descriptive Title:* usually the same used on the petition; some statutes may have an official title but be popularly known by the name of a person who inspired the initiative (e.g., "Megan's Law," named after Megan Kanka, a 7-year-old New Jersey girl whose murder by a twice-convicted sex offender inspired the federal Sex Offender Registration Act)
>
> *Summary:* short description of the law's purpose and rationale
>
> *Provisions:* single-spaced and arranged in outline form, first by letters with sub-sections numbered

CONSTITUTIONAL AMENDMENT PETITION FORM

104.185 – A person who knowingly signs a petition or petitions for a candidate, a minor political party, or an issue more than one time commits a misdemeanor of the first degree, punishable as provided in s.775.082 or s.775.083.

TITLE: *Animal Cruelty Amendment: Limiting Cruel and Inhumane Confinement of Pigs During Pregnancy*

SUMMARY: Inhumane treatment of animals is a concern of Florida citizens; to prevent cruelty to animals and as recommended by The Humane Society of the United States, no person shall confine a pig during pregnancy in a cage, crate or other enclosure, or tether a pregnant pig, on a farm so that the pig is prevented from turning around freely, except for veterinary purposes and during the prebirthing period; provides definitions, penalties, and an effective date.

I am a registered voter of Florida and hereby petition the Secretary of State to place the following amendment to the Florida Constitution on the ballot in the general election.

Is this a change of address for your voter registration? ☐ YES ☐ NO

Name_____
(Please print name as it appears on voter I.D. card)

Street Address_____

City_____ Zip_____

County_____

Voter Registration Number_____
- or -
Date of Birth _____/_____/_____.

✖ _____ Date_____
Signature of Registered Voter   Date Signed

FULL TEXT OF PROPOSED AMENDMENT: BE IT ENACTED BY THE PEOPLE OF FLORIDA THAT:

Article X, Section 19, Florida Constitution, is hereby created to read as follows:
Limiting Cruel and Inhumane Confinement of Pigs During Pregnancy.

Inhumane treatment of animals is a concern of Florida citizens. To prevent cruelty to certain animals and as recommended by The Humane Society of the United States, the people of the State of Florida hereby limit the cruel and inhumane confinement of pigs during pregnancy as provided herein.

(a) It shall be unlawful for any person to confine a pig during pregnancy in an enclosure, or to tether a pig during pregnancy, on a farm in such a way that she is prevented from turning around freely.

(b) This section shall not apply:
  (1) when a pig is undergoing an examination, test, treatment or operation carried out for veterinary purposes, provided the period during which the animal is confined or tethered is not longer than reasonably necessary.
  (2) during the prebirthing period.

(c) For purposes of this section:
  (1) "enclosure" means any cage, crate or other enclosure in which a pig is kept for all or the majority of any day, including what is commonly described as the "gestation crate."
  (2) "farm" means the land, buildings, support facilities, and other appurtenances used in the production of animals for food or fiber.
  (3) "person" means any natural person, corporation and/or business entity.
  (4) "pig" means any animal of the porcine species.
  (5) "turning around freely" means turning around without having to touch any side of the pig's enclosure.
  (6) "prebirthing period" means the seven day period prior to a pig's expected date of giving birth.

(d) A person who violates this section shall be guilty of a misdemeanor of the first degree, punishable as provided in s. 775.082(4)(a), Florida Statutes (1999), as amended, or by a fine of not more than $5000, or by both imprisonment and a fine, unless and until the legislature enacts more stringent penalties for violations hereof. On and after the effective date of this section, law enforcement officers in the state are authorized to enforce the provisions of this section in the same manner and authority as if a violation of this section constituted a violation of Section 828.13, Florida Statutes (1999). The confinement or tethering of each pig shall constitute a separate offense. The knowledge or acts of agents and employees of a person in regard to a pig owned, farmed or in the custody of a person, shall be held to be the knowledge or act of such person.

(e) It is the intent of this section that implementing legislation is not required for enforcing any violations hereof.

(f) If any portion of this section is held invalid for any reason, the remaining portion of this section, to the fullest extent possible, shall be severed from the void portion and given the fullest possible force and application.

(g) This section shall take effect six years after approval by the electors.

RETURN TO: Floridians for Humane Farms
1859 South Dixie Highway
Pompano Beach, FL 33060
(954)946-1691

For Office Use Only:
Serial Number: _____00-06_____
Date Approved: _____10-27-00_____

Pd. pol. adv. by Floridians for Humane Farms

Figure 9.2. This state-level petition seeks to place a controversial measure on the ballot for voters to approve or reject. While some petitions must be signed in the presence of a canvasser, this one can be privately considered and sent to the organization spearheading the petition drive.[3]

Statute: a precise statement of what the proposed legislation mandates

Exceptions/Exemptions: individuals, conditions, or situations to which the law does not apply

Definitions: clarifies any confusing or potentially ambiguous language that might open legislative loopholes

Enforcement: penalties for violation

Timeline: when the law will take effect

Other: any additional information related to the enforceability or constitutionality of the proposed legislation

You don't need a law degree to write ballot initiatives. Government staff and many nonprofit organizations are available to help citizens convert their ideas for action into legally binding documents. Still, no legislative process comes to fruition through the efforts of a single person, and since the stakes for ballot initiatives are so high, it's wise to consult a lawyer or experienced government writer as you work with civic documents (and it can't hurt to familiarize yourself with your city's charter or state's constitution).

Some people have expressed concern that if anyone can submit a ballot initiative, then the civic process can be reduced to a series of "neverendums" dominated by special interest groups. It's certainly true that some individuals and groups have the resources to hire lawyers and campaign consultants to persuade voters to support their ballot initiatives; indeed, it's not unheard of for initiatives to be passed into law exactly as proposed. This kind of success is of course satisfying for the initiative's sponsors and supporters, but it also raises questions about the degree to which legislation truly represents the public interest.

Government participation should be accessible to everyone, not just well-funded interest groups. The fact of the matter is that most ballot initiatives fail. But like petitions, they remain one of the few genres that maintains the public's access to representative governance.

Exercise

Consult the website for The Ballot Initiative Strategy Center (*http://www.ballot.org*) to find out whether your state allows citizens to propose ballot initiatives. If it does, research the rules, procedures, and deadlines governing this process, and check the status of any ballot initiatives pending in your state. If you are interested in supporting any of these efforts, write down contact information in your writer's notebook and follow up later.

If your state does not allow ballot initiatives, choose a state that does and do the same research. If you believe your state should allow such initiatives, consider writing a letter of concern to your state representative urging him or her to initiate this change through a ballot referendum.

Peer Review

Before writing a petition or undertaking a ballot initiative, you should work through the "Thinking Rhetorically" checklists in Chapters 3 and 4 to make sure that these are appropriate responses to an urgent rhetorical situation. Before submitting your documents to a rhetorical audience, you should ask someone you trust to read it with the following questions in mind:

- Does the writer have a clear and detailed understanding of the government processes in which this document will participate? Is s/he aware of all rules, procedures, or deadlines that are required parts of this process?

- What is the purpose of this document? Does it clearly and concisely identify the problem and explain why the writer finds this situation urgent? Does it request a specific, feasible action?

- Does the document address an appropriate rhetorical audience?

- How would you characterize the language, tone, and style of the document? Are these appropriate to its audience and purpose? Does it include accurate information, with a minimum of emotional appeals?

- In the case of petitions, how will the document solicit signatures? Does this method seem appropriate and effective?

- In the case of non-binding petitions, does the draft conform to the conventions of open letters or letters of concern (see Chapter 6)?

- In the case of legally binding petitions, does the draft include all information necessary for the validation of signatures? Does this information fit on a single page?

- Does the draft identify and provide contact information for its sponsor? Does the sponsoring individual or group sound credible?

- After reading the petition or ballot initiative, are you inclined to support it with your signature or vote? Why or why not?

- Is there anything in the petition or ballot initiative that strikes you as especially wrong, uninformed, inappropriate, offensive, or suspect? If so, what?

- If there are any problems, how might they be addressed in a revision?

Petitions in Action

Pedro and some friends were concerned that their favorite live music venue, the Fire-belly Lounge, had been cited repeatedly for violation of the city noise ordinance and was in danger of being shut down (see Chapter 5). They conducted on-line research on this issue and learned that the ordinance had been adopted only recently and re-mained controversial—mainly for its use of noise meters that were so imprecise that they could not accurately measure whether decibel limits were being exceeded, leaving individual police officers to determine whether a noise sounded "too loud." As a con-sequence, enforcement of the ordinance was erratic at best.

Sec. 6-28.1. Measurement of sound level.

In determining sound levels pursuant to this article, the standards, instrumentation, personnel, measurement procedures, and reporting procedures shall be as specified herein; and all terminology not defined herein or in section 6-27 shall be in conformance with the American National Standards Institute (ANSI).

(a)   Sound level measurement shall be made with a sound level meter using the A-weighting scale, set on slow response.

(b)   Sound level meters shall be serviced, calibrated and operated as recommended by the manufacturer and in accordance with regulations prescribed by the police department. Persons using the sound level meter shall be trained in sound level measurement and the operation of sound level measuring equipment.

(c)   Except as otherwise specified, sound level measurements shall be made from within the boundary line of any improved and occupied property; where this is impracticable, the measurement shall be taken at the exterior wall of the principal structure on such property. In the case of an elevated or directional sound, compliance with the prescribed limits shall be required at any elevation on the property.

(d)   Except as specified in (g) below, the sound measurement shall be averaged over a period of at least one (1) minute for purposes of determining the sound level. Sound levels may not exceed the prescribed level by more than three (3) decibels at any time during the measurement period.

(e)   During measurement, the microphone shall not be positioned so as to create any unnatural enhancement of the measured sound. A windscreen shall be used when appropriate.

(f)   Traffic noise and noise from other sources not connected with the sound being measured shall not be considered in taking measurements.

(g)   In the case of noise that is impulsive or is not continuous, the measurement shall be taken over a period of time of at least one (1) minute. Any such sound or noise that exceeds the prescribed level more than two (2) times in a minute shall be deemed to exceed the prescribed sound levels.

(h)   In the case of outdoor entertainment, including live or recorded speech, music, or other sound, whether or not a permit is required for the activity under section 6-30(b)(1), sound level measurements shall be made as prescribed in this section. In no case, however, shall the decibel level of such activity exceed the levels allowed pursuant to this article when measured at a point one hundred (100) feet away from the source of the sound and beyond the boundary line of the premises from which the noise emanates.

(Ord. of 10-19-93, § 2.c)

Figure 9.3. Pedro's group examined all laws, statutes, and ordinances related to the local noise ordinance as they considered possible actions in support of their favorite bar. Although these documents can be difficult to decipher, they can also reveal opportunities for civic action.

Further research revealed a number of exceptions to the ordinance, including noise from street fairs, "lawful" fireworks, and film and video productions for which permits have been issued. Knowing this, Pedro and his friends decided to circulate a petition requesting exemptions for businesses which had been operating lawfully in the city since before the current noise ordinance was approved.

In researching the rules and procedures for bringing petitions before the City Council, Pedro learned that his group needed to demonstrate that residents of at least 51% of the homes in the affected area must approve of the proposal. This led him to the City Attorney to find a legal definition of "affected area" and the Office of City Planning to obtain a map and determine the boundaries of this area. Since the City Council meets biweekly, Pedro learned that the petition had no firm deadline; however, in order to be placed on the agenda for consideration by the Council it had to be submitted to administrative offices at least five business days in advance of the meeting. Pedro would be allowed ten minutes to present his proposal to the Council and was advised to come prepared with copies of relevant documents for each of the seven Council members.

The petition draft that Pedro brought to his group for peer review appears below. Consult the guidelines for writing petitions and the peer review questions listed above, then read the petition carefully. If you were as concerned as Pedro about the fate of the Fire-belly Lounge, what suggestions would you offer him as he undertakes his revisions?

PETITION TO EXEMPT BUSINESSES FROM NOISE ORDINANCE

Local ordinances regulating noise must balance the needs of residents with the needs of businesses. The undersigned hereby petition the City of Herndon to exempt from their noise ordinances any lawfully operating business that has been in operation since before the current noise ordinance went into effect.

Name	Address	Signature	Tel. #

The contact person for this petition is
Pedro Marques, 5049 14th Ave. S., 822-2464.

Return all petition forms to:
City of Herndon Clerk's Office
P.O. Box 3297, Herndon, VA 20172-0427

Please make a copy of this petition for you records.

Notes

1. Fryer, Bronwyn, and Lakshmi Chaudhry. "<Fwd: Fwd: Re: Read This Now." Mother Jones March/April 1999. July 2002. <http://www.motherjones.com/mother_jones/MA99/fryerand-chaudhry.html>.

2. *The Civic Mind.* July 2002. The Civic Mind. <http://www.civicmind.com/ballot>. *The Ballot Initiative Strategy Center.* 20 June 2002. The Ballot Initiative Strategy Center. July 2002. <http://www.ballot.org>.

3. *Ban Cruel Farms.* July 2002. Floridians for Humane Farms. <http://www.bancruel-farms.org>.

CHAPTER 10

Public Literacy, Community Service, and Activism

Up until now, the primary focus of this book has been how to participate in public literacy as an individual acting in what you believe to be the public interest. In these last two chapters we will explore opportunites to participate in public literacy in the context of more organized groups: in this chapter, through community service and activism, and in Chapter 11, on the job.

In 1859, educator Horace Mann exhorted the graduating class of Antioch College to "be ashamed to die until you have won some victory of humanity." More than a century later, Marian Wright Edelman, founder and president of the Children's Defense Fund, said that "Service is the rent we pay for living." In other words (at least according to these two social reformers), making the world a better place is the obligation of everyone. But community service and activism require more than just a feeling of "duty"—more, even, than a passion for justice or a desire to help. They also call for reflection on motives, goals, and skills. This chapter will address these issues and explore three kinds of community service you can pursue through public literacy: volunteering, service learning, and grassroots organizing.

Thinking About Service

Community service describes organized, generally uncompensated actions that support or enhance the quality of life in a community. These actions are usually voluntary (an exception is when people are required to perform community service after being convicted of crimes), and most people engage in them because they want to share their talents or resources with others. Community service implies an investment of time and effort rather than simply money or moral support. It often evolves out of the attitude that we are responsible for solving shared problems—even if we're busy and our contributions are modest.

Community service responds to urgent—sometimes life or death—situations. Some urgent problems call for actions that are purely physical, such as building a house or delivering meals to the homebound. Others are rhetorical situations that invite discursive action in the form of public literacy. Identifying the urgent needs of a community includes recognizing problems and determining whether they can best be addressed through community service or some other means.

It is important to think of community service as a relationship as well as a set of actions. It involves you and other members of a community in a partnership that comes at the invitation of the community and that the community believes is important and useful. Developing this kind of relationship requires attention to local knowledge, including local needs and opportunities; a willingness to learn from those you serve, as opposed to a misguided sense of yourself as "savior"; and in most cases, a long-term commitment to the issue, the setting, or the people you wish to serve.

Before getting involved in community service, you should evaluate your motives as honestly as possible. If they are purely self interested—for example, improving your job prospects, gaining the admiration of others, or fulfilling a requirement for school—you may actually alienate the people whom you are trying to help, creating a negative environment for everyone involved. At the same time, personal interests can be compatible with public interests (see Chapter 1), so if you genuinely want to improve a situation, even in a small way—and even if you expect some personal benefits as well—you might be well suited to this kind of work.

Upon his retirement from the U. S. Supreme Court, Justice Thurgood Marshall remarked, "I did what I could with what I had." This is the essence of community service: figuring out what you like to do and what you do well, then finding or creating opportunities to put those skills to work toward meaningful projects in the public interest.

Volunteering

The most common form of community service is probably *volunteering*: unpaid labor willingly given. You might already have experience with volunteering in the form of tutoring, assisting with political campaigns, working as a museum docent, coaching a youth soccer team, or participating in a clean-up effort. If so, you probably chose to do this work because you had a personal interest in the issue, wanted to get some professional experience, or just thought it would be fun.

If you've never volunteered before, you might legitimately wonder why anyone would bother to work without pay. It's true that volunteering can be mentally and physically exhausting, especially if you are also going to school, working, and caring for a family. But in addition to the satisfaction of knowing that they have contributed to some project in the public interest, most volunteers also report a multitude of personal benefits from their actions, including feeling more connected to the people around them and becoming more understanding and tolerant of differences. Some actually change the direction of their lives and careers as a result of their efforts, and most feel that they "get back" at least as much as they give.

Public writing is one way to volunteer. Many nonprofit organizations and advocacy groups need people who are confident and versatile writers for public audiences and purposes—people who know how to write effective letters, flyers, grant proposals, and other documents. Such groups often publish their own magazines or newsletters and may need people who can research and write articles as well.

Most organizations ask potential volunteers to fill out an application before putting them to work. This allows the group to make good use of the applicant's skills while still meeting their own needs. If you are interested in public writing, say so on your application, but don't be discouraged if your supervisors don't immediately put you to work writing petitions. Usually volunteers start out by learning a variety of duties, skills, and procedures so that they can become more familiar with the mission of the group they're working for. This kind of experience might initially seem unrelated to public writing, but in fact it's a kind of research: the more you know about the goals and resources of your group, the more effective you can be in recognizing urgent rhetorical situations and responding to them appropriately.

Most communities offer a wide variety of volunteer opportunities so that any potential volunteer can find something of interest. Some communities have agencies that coordinate the volunteer needs of several organizations; if no such agency exists in your community, you can simply call or visit the agency you are interested in working for. Information about volunteering opportunities can usually be found in the phone book, at the Chamber of Commerce or United Way, in local newspapers, and on the Internet. Your campus might also have an office that can direct students to community agencies in need of volunteers.

Service Learning

The goal of *service learning* is to produce civic-minded students who not only think critically about social problems but also take actions to solve them. Toward that end, service learning courses teach academic knowledge and skills in the context of community service projects or some other form of experiential learning. Students earn course credit by applying their learning to some effort in the public interest, usually in collaboration with members of the local community.

Service learning manifests the same ideals of civic education that we considered in Chapter 1. However, it also attempts to intervene in a longstanding problem in the United States: indifferent or even hostile relations between universities and their host communities. Since many students (and faculty) are not native to the cities where they attend school, they may see themselves as temporary residents, without any particular investment in the community at large. Service learning assumes that members of a university community are also members of a local community and thus responsible for its welfare. This includes sharing university resources like libraries, computer facilities, and the expert knowledge and skills that can help solve local problems or advance local interests.

Service learning programs have been developed in many disciplines, including nursing, business, education, and the natural sciences. And while these programs often involve professional outreach (e.g., helping residents with their taxes, running a vaccination clinic), they almost always make extensive use of writing, such as creating authentic public documents on behalf of community groups. Students in a communications class, for example, created a website and public service announcement on behalf of the local Humane Society, as well as a series of flyers that they posted around campus.

PERSONALS

Homeless puppy seeking loving owner. Enjoys playing catch, likes children, and long walks on the beach

Don't let lives end, save a furry friend.

Support the New Hanover Humane Society
call 763-6692 or visit http://humanesociety.wilmington.org
Sponsored by COM 467 Students of UNCW

Figure 10.1. This flyer was created by a group of college students as part of their coursework for a communications class. In addition to helping the students apply their academic learning, the project assisted the local Humane Society in promoting pet adoptions.

In most service learning situions, people are really counting on your writing to assist them in efforts that are important to them and that may directly affect their lives. The "real world" implications of service writing can thus invigorate your academic work with a new sense of purpose, motivate you to do a good job and meet deadlines, and provide you with opportunities to write for audiences other than teachers and peers.

But service learning also poses many potential challenges, which include everything from logistical difficulties (e.g., scheduling conflicts) to inconsistent messages about what constitutes "good writing." As with community service in general, participants in service learning projects must consciously resist the role of "do-gooder." It's fine to feel a sense of pride and satisfaction from your contributions, but if these good feelings create resentment among the people you're assisting or interfere with the effectiveness of your interaction, then it's time to re-evaluate your motives.

Although it can be difficult to foster relationships in which different constituencies see each other as partners with shared interests, such efforts are supported by several national as well as local public documents. In 1993, for example, President Bill Clinton signed the National Community Trust Act, which encourages states to develop programs that link schools and communities in joint endeavors to solve social problems. Your campus might have an office that sponsors such endeavors, and individual professors may also develop service learning initiatives. Finally, some internships provide opportunities for service learning; working with an advocacy group, community literacy office, or government agency could offer an invaluable apprenticeship in public literacy. Chapter 11 describes several careers whose focus is writing in the public interest.

Thinking about Activism

Activism is the politically astute cousin of service. Both of these approaches to community problem solving share a commitment to advancing public interests, but two important differences exist. First, activism generally concerns itself with injustices rather than problems—that is, things that are unfair as opposed to simply unfortunate. Second, activism goes to the root of those injustices (which is why activists are sometimes called "radicals") while service seeks to help victims of those injustices without necessarily addressing the larger social forces that create their problems.

Of course, one person's problem is another person's injustice; therefore neither activism nor service should be regarded as "better" or more important. Both strengthen our communities in vital, often inspiring ways, and some people find it worthwhile to engage in both. However, because they serve different needs, activism and service also require different sorts of skills and perspectives.

Consider the issue of homelessness, for example. People interested in addressing this issue through community service would probably be most concerned with assisting homeless individuals in meeting their basic requirements for food, clothing, and shelter. Toward that end, they might work at a soup kitchen or food pantry, coordinate social services such as job training, or help build homes with the local chapter of Habitat for Humanity. Activists, on the other hand, would be more likely to target the institutional or systemic factors that cause people to become homeless. Their energies, then, might be focused on ensuring that all workers are paid a living wage or lobbying for better public health care for the mentally ill.

It would be exhausting (not to mention depressing) to mobilize around every issue that matters to us, but it's possible to be an activist in different ways depending on your resources and level of commitment. For example, some issues might motivate you to invest a great deal of time, creativity, or personal resources, while others might rate only some spare change in a donation bucket, a vote at the ballot box, or a "Right on!" to protesters. It's also possible to be an "organic" activist—that is, to ask questions about the world and respond through appropriate actions not just within the context of organized events, but simply as a way of living your life. Seen in this way, activism represents a way of taking ownership of your ideals for how the world should be.

Ultimately, though, activism requires more than idealism. It requires you to think critically about power as well as to access the power that's in front of you. Since change rarely happens overnight, it also requires you to be satisfied with small accomplishments achieved over a long period of time. Finally, activism needs to be accountable to a constituency, move beyond rants and accusations into the realm of purposeful actions, and work with a certain level of efficiency and impact. Otherwise, you are doomed to be a lone crusader toiling away at "random acts of protest."

In recent years, massive rallies—mostly protesting globalism and many involving college students—have made activism look almost glamorous. In truth, the people and efforts that are responsible for most social changes rarely make the cover of *Newsweek*. Still, things happen only when people make them happen, and the history of the world is filled with previously unassuming people who took bold action when circumstances demanded it. Why not you?

Grassroots Organizing

Sometimes people have an interest in activism or community service but can't find a group whose interests and goals are consistent with their own. Or sometimes an urgent situation arises for which no organized advocacy group yet exists. If you perceive a gap in the community service or activism opportunities at your school or in your community, you might consider organizing a group yourself; FACT of Life (see Chapters 4 and 8) and SCAT (see Chapter 4) emerged under these very circumstances.

Grassroots organizing describes the efforts on the part of members of everyday and local public spheres to mobilize around some public interest, in effect creating activism or community service opportunities for themselves and likeminded partners. Often these efforts respond to very specific, very urgent problems, such as the misconduct of an elected official or the threatened demolition of a beloved local landmark. Some grassroots organizations simply disband as these situations are improved or become less urgent, while others continually evolve, modifying their missions in order to address new problems and concerns that arise.

Local and campus communities are filled with grassroots organizations—some very prominent and well established, others loosely organized and transient. In one small town in North Carolina, for example, citizens formed a group called Concerned Citizens of Southport to oppose the building of a large Wal-Mart store in their community. Although these efforts were ultimately unsuccessful, the group is still active in its community, having expanded its focus to include issues related to urban development, taxation, and the environment.

The Sweat-Free Campus Campaign began when students realized that their universities were profiting from garment industry sweatshops. Through carefully coordinated publicity efforts, students have raised awareness about this issue on campuses across the country, persuading officials at several universities to adopt a Code of Conduct that obligates them to take responsibility for the conditions under which their licensed apparel is made. In only a few years, the campaign has grown into an international organization: the United Students Against Sweatshops (USAS), with chapters on over 200 campuses as well as a newletter (*Re:Act*), a conference, and a significantly expanded agenda.

Grassroots organizations distinguish themselves by starting from scratch—"from the ground up." They represent groups of people working to help themselves and their own communities rather than waiting for someone else to do it. The student government organization or leadership center on your campus might offer support for grassroots organizing on campus. Other excellent resources include the following:

> *Vancouver Citizens Committee*: supports individuals and organizations in building and maintaining public spaces on the Internet; publishes *The Citizen's Handbook*
>
> > http://www.vcn.bc.ca/citizens-handbook/

> *Protest.net*: an activist collective working to create alternative media; publishes a downloadable *Activists Handbook* and two magazines—*ZNet* and *Freedom Writer*—whose articles are archived on the Web
>
> > http://www.protest.net

> *@Grass-Roots.org*: a clearinghouse for information about small, innovative grassroots organizations
>
> > http://www.grass-roots.org

> *Get Active*: sponsored by Greenpeace Australia; includes information on public speaking, lobbying politicians and corporations, working with the media, starting a website, and much more
>
> > http://www.greenpeace.org.au/getactive/

These websites include extensive links to grassroots as well as national and international advocacy groups; a variety of downloadable documents, publications, and graphics; calendars of events; and more. Some will create links to your group's website, publicize your events, and otherwise assist you in your activist efforts. If none of these organizations has what you're looking for, you can find other information simply by typing the words *grassroots organizing* into any search engine or consulting most advocacy websites.

Exercise

Look through your writer's notebook and make a list of interests or concerns that you would like to be more actively involved in. Brainstorm the names of any organizations that share your interests, then look on-line and in local and campus directories for agencies or organizations that might share your interests, an "umbrella" agency that coordinates volunteer efforts for several groups, or an Internet portal that contains links to affiliated sites. Write down their names and contact information, and find out what community service opportunities are available.

Then, find out if there is an office that coordinates service learning efforts at your school. If there is, locate professors who offer service learning courses and ask them about the kinds of projects they have worked on; write down this information in your writer's notebook for future reference. If there isn't an organized service learning program, approach one of your professors to propose a service learning project as part of your semester grade. You might, for example, ask your women's studies professor if you could create a public information kit for the local rape crisis center as your final class project instead of writing a research paper.

In addition to women's health issues, one of Summer's most pressing concerns is overpopulation. Although she didn't find any local organizations that dealt with this issue, she found several national and international groups, including *http://www.overpopulation.com*, -.org, and -.net. Through the Population Connection website Summer located several internship opportunities at organizations advocating for sound population and immigration policies. However, because these opportunities were not geographically feasible for her, she decided to pursue service learning opportunities locally, through her campus leadership center.

Case in Point: Cyber-Activism

It's not an exaggeration to say that the Internet has revolutionized activism and that activism has, in turn, revitalized public literacy. New technologies have made it possible to communicate with millions of people simultaneously at no cost; websites represent virtual public spheres that are at once geographically stable and geographically immaterial, a place where visitors can find you at any time of day, from practically anywhere in the world.

Activists have not only adapted traditional public discourse genres such as appeal letters and press kits, but they have also literally invented new genres that are well suited to this new public sphere. In fact, technological sophistication has become so important among 21st-century activists that the Ruckus Society, a group that trains environmental and human rights activists in the skills of nonviolent civil disobedience, organized its 2002 Summer Action Camp around the theme "Tech Toolbox Action Camp." According to the group's website, *www.ruckus.org*, the purpose of the camp is to find ways to use technology as effectively and creatively as possible; toward that end, it offers workshops on technical skills, electronic organizing, independent media, and secure collaboration.

One of the new genres invented by activist groups is the *action alert*—an electronic bulletin that informs audience members of an urgent situation (often a rhetorical situation) and requests an immediate, specific response. Action alerts are delivered via e-mail to a subscriber list and typically announce upcoming legislative actions that concerned citizens might be able to influence. The activist equivalent of a news flash, action alerts are not the best genre to build gradual support for an issue or cause. For example, in an effort to influence the passage of legislation banning snowmobiles in national parks, organizations representing environmentalists and outdoor sports enthusiasts circulated action alerts asking subscribers to contact legislators and sign an online petition. Like most action alerts, this one dealt with the immediate and short-term; it had a very specific goal and a non-negotiable deadline.

As their name suggests, action alerts are succinct texts and generally contain the same sorts of information: a brief (two to three paragraphs) summary of the issue, a summary of the organization's position, and a request for specific action(s). Local or every-day groups are more likely to ask their audiences to attend a rally or other gathering (e.g., City Council meeting) to demonstrate their support for a cause. National or global groups, however—such as Amnesty International or the National Coalition for the Homeless—typically use action alerts to ask their rhetorical audience to write a letter, sign a petition, or contact politicians.

Because nonprofit groups are more likely to have an office staff and at least a few paid employees, these action alerts often include links to more detailed information, such as reports and articles, the websites of associated groups, and so on; they may provide form letters or suggestions on how to write an effective letter of concern. Most organizations decline to copyright these resources and in fact encourage members of their audience to download them, forward them to other people, and even use them verbatim without attribution when taking action in the public interest (see Chapter 1).

Part One: Studying the Genre

Phil Agre, a professor of Information Studies at the University of California, Los Angeles, has compiled a set of guidelines for "Designing Effective Action Alerts for the Internet"; this can be found at dlis.gseis.ucla.edu/people/pagre/alerts.html. Consult the site, and if possible print out the suggestions. Then, alone or in small groups, return to the advocacy websites you examined in the previous exercise (or simply type action alerts into any search engine). Look at some "real life" action alerts and consider the following questions:

- In general, do action alerts tend to adhere to the guidelines recommended by Professor Agre? In what ways, if any, do they differ? Do those differences confuse or otherwise undermine the message? After looking at several action alerts, would you add any suggestions to Professor Agre's list?

- What strategies do the action alerts use to invoke a rhetorical audience? How effective are these strategies, in your opinion? In the process of your investigation, did you respond to any of the action alerts or sign up for any of the mailing lists? Why or why not?

- Besides action alerts, what other strategies or genres do advocacy organizations use to get audiences involved in their causes? In what ways are these strategies and genres specific to the on-line public sphere, and in what ways are they simply adaptations of more traditional genres?

Part Two: Critical Reflection

The website Two-Minute Activist (http://capwiz.com/aauw.index) is dedicated to the idea that it takes very little time or effort to advocate productively for a cause: one minute to learn about an issue and one minute to act on it. Some people, however, believe that the Internet makes activism too easy. In other words, if taking action requires little more than the click of a mouse, then people might be less willing to undertake the equally necessary but more challenging actions such as writing a grant proposal or organizing (or attending) a protest. Most on-line actions—signing a petition, for example—neither require nor particularly encourage any longterm commitment to an issue or cause. As discussed in Chapter 9, some can have unintended consequences.

The danger, then, is that electronic activism can make people *feel* as if they're taking action when in fact they're becoming more passive. Still, many activists believe that any level of commitment is better than none, and that constant reminders that an issue needs support can incrementally influence audiences to get more involved. What do you think?

Look again at the advocacy websites that you've found, this time with the following questions in mind:

- What opportunities for action (rhetorical or otherwise) do the organizations provide? How might these opportunities meet the needs of audiences with different skills, resources, and levels of commitment?

- In what ways do advocacy organizations encourage longterm commitment from members of their audience?

You might also take a look at the Two-Minute Activist site and assess its overall purpose and effectiveness.

CHAPTER 11

Careers in Public Literacy

As this book mentioned earlier, there are many ways to participate in public literacy professionally. Journalism, advertising, public relations, and law are examples of professions whose practitioners create a variety of public documents on a regular basis. In general, though, these professions are limited to people who have college degrees or professional licenses authorizing them to do that work.

There are, however, many other careers that require writing for public audiences and purposes but do not require a particular degree or license. In other words, these careers are available to non-specialists. This chapter introduces you to some of these careers, as well as to people who are involved in them. Many of the people profiled here had no prior experience with public literacy but entered their careers because of their commitment to issues in the public interest. Many of them, moreover, started out as volunteers or interns before becoming full-time employees.

Grant Writer

Patty Chase is the Grants and Budget Director for Friendship Home in Lincoln, Nebraska, a shelter for domestic violence victims and their children. In addition to monitoring her agency's budget, Chase is responsible for preparing all grant proposals that are submitted to various local, state, and national funding sources. As part of her grant writing duties, she researches potential funding sources, meets with staff in order to keep apprised of programmatic needs, and writes all proposals. Chase was a psychology major in college, and since writing papers was a major part of her coursework, she learned the benefits of good research and preparation, being organized and getting things done on time—all of which can mean the difference between a successful and unsuccessful proposal.

Chase's first position at Friendship Home was Children's Program Coordinator, where she was responsible for providing services for the children living at the shelter. Consequently, her first motives for grant writing were, she claims, "strictly personal": finding support to hire an assistant. Buoyed by her successful achievement of this goal, she became "hooked" on writing grants. And although Chase now has several years of grant writing experience, she believes that "there is always room for improvement and modification," and so continues to search for ways to convey information more effectively in the proposals she writes. One important lesson Chase has learned about writing in the public interest is that proposals must explain how the project is going to benefit the women and children served by her agency, not the agency itself.

A typical day for Chase includes writing and conducting research for information she needs to complete her proposals; this might range from finding statistics to calling vendors for price estimates. Chase admits that it can be difficult to make the same information sound compelling, and so it's tempting to get complacent and submit the same proposal over and over again to different funders. Despite these challenges, Chase knows that her work helps to keep women and children safe in times of crisis. She says, "That's what keeps me wanting to learn more about how to be a better grant writer."

Public Information Officer

Larry Kamholz is the Public Information Officer for the Madison, Wisconsin, Police Department. As liaison between the police and the local community, his job is to promote a positive image of the department, educate the public about issues related to crime and law enforcement, and assist members of the media in doing their work. To facilitate these efforts he writes press releases, departmental memos, and a bimonthly newsletter; posts information on the department website; fills out internal paperwork; and communicates with various constituents via telephone and e-mail.

This is Kamholz's ninth year in law enforcement. Before becoming a PIO he earned a degree in police science from a technical college, then served as a patrol officer and in the traffic bureau. Although he has had no special training in public writing, participating in high school public speaking contests and, later, in volunteer organizations has taught Kamholz how to set aside his own perspectives in order to anticipate what other people want to know. He respects his audience and does all he can to give them interesting, accurate, timely information.

Kamholz starts each workday by reading the dispatch logs and officers' reports for the past 24 hours so that he is prepared to field requests for information from local citizens, media outlets, and others. The most challenging part of Kamholz's job is negotiating the "information gap" between the police and the media, since he must be sensitive to investigations while still providing the media with enough information to satisfy the public interest. On the other hand, being a PIO gives Kamholz the opportunity to show people how much police contribute to the community, which is why—in addition to his other duties—he participates in two "ask the cop" radio shows and speaks regularly to community groups.

It bothers Kamholz that the most prominent image of police officers is often a negative one, and he considers it a personal mission to humanize law enforcement officers.

One way he accomplishes this is through press releases. Kamholz admits that his early press releases were uniformly serious and filled with police jargon. Now that he is more comfortable writing in this genre, he finds that he is able to incorporate his own voice and sense of humor, when appropriate (see Figure 11.1). Of course, his audience lets him know if he takes this too far, and Kamholz is grateful for the negative feedback as well as the positive, because it teaches him how to do his job better and gives him insight into who the public is and how to communicate with them effectively.

Madison Police Department

Press Release for Case Number 2002-51531

INCIDENT:	Injured Person
CASE NUMBER:	2002-51531
ADDRESS:	700 Dexter St.
DATE:	5/11/2002
CASE TIME:	8:04 AM
ARRESTED PERSON/SUSPECT:	N/A
VICTIM/INJURIES:	41 year old male from Madison. Claimed of minor aches and pains and was transported to a local hospital for treatment.
DETAILS OF INCIDENT:	Officers were dispatched to the 700 block of Dexter St. on May 11th around 8:00am for an injured person. Officers, along with Fire and Rescue responded and located the 41 year old victim who had apparently fell from a two story balcony. According to the 41 year old victim, two of his female friends were walking towards his apartment to come and socialize with him. The excited 41 year old, decided to get up on his balcony railing and cheer on the two oncoming friends. The problem - an unknown, unidentified bird, who thought the 41 year old was hailing it, came swooping down at the victim causing the 41 year old to lose his balance and fall to the ground below. The bird fled from the scene and was unavailable for questioning. The 41 year old was transported to a local hospital for non life threatening injuries.
DATE OF RELEASE:	5/13/2002
TIME OF RELEASE:	9:51 AM
RELEASED BY:	PIO Larry Kamholz

Figure 11.1. As this press release draft illustrates, even the most formulaic public genres can make use of personal voice. Do you think the author has gone too far with his sense of humor?

Community Literacy Director

Katie Morrow is the Program Coordinator for the Cape Fear Literacy Council in Wilmington, North Carolina, where she is responsible for almost all the writing that comes out of the organization, including grants, newsletters, appeal letters, reports, general correspondence, and tutor training materials. Currently she is also conducting an informal research project that examines the effect of innovative tutoring methods with learning disabled clients. Previously, Morrow worked as an information officer at Oxfam, an international hunger relief organization.

Morrow was an art history major in college, but decided not to pursue a career in this field after working as a guard at the Hirshhorn Museum in Washington, D.C. one summer. The student workers, all of whom were white, worked alongside full-time security guards, all of whom were black Vietnam veterans. Once she began observing a variety of disparities in their working conditions—including pay scales, office space, and schedules—Morrow said, "It was impossible to avoid social justice issues." So she worked as a volunteer for several organizations after graduating and getting married, and she later got a full-time job at Oxfam.

Morrow perceives three public spheres in her current position: the donors and potential donors whose names are on their mailing list; newspaper readers and the news media, who spread the word about the Literacy Council's services; and the Council's clients, who are primarily people who don't read or respond to the mail and require very different types of communication. The complexities of public writing have made Morrow keenly interested in readability issues, particularly "how we create a genuine public space for people who are illiterate or semiliterate." Through her work at Oxfam and the Literacy Council, she has become aware that the words she uses and the ways in which she writes determine who will have access to her message.

Because her writing at Oxfam was "internal"—directed toward employees of the organization—Morrow describes it as "very safe." The writing she does for the Literacy Council goes to "the outside world," and so she's never sure how (or whether) her audience will respond. She admits, though, that "There's a power" to writing that is linked to actions that make a difference in people's lives. This is a lesson her clients are learning, too, as they write short essays for the organization's newsletter, The Challenger. Morrow finds that as she works with people who are learning to read and write, the motives and agendas they bring to their literacy give her insight into her own work.

Fund Raiser

Barb Weismann is a development director for the Seattle Public Theater, where she performs and supervises all tasks related to fund raising. Her responsibilities include writing grant proposals (on average, one a week); writing appeal letters to potential donors; developing themes for fund raising campaigns, and writing the text for brochures and various marketing documents. She also writes thank you letters to grant funders and corresponds with people requesting information about her organization. Weismann wrote her first grants as a volunteer for a homeless shelter, which then hired her to raise money for an elevator renovation.

Weismann reports that the most challenging and gratifying aspect of her job is "finding out what works": coming up with new ideas to solve problems and start projects, and figuring out what will give people the incentive to support her organization financially.

Through her experience, Weismann has this advice for people interested in public writing. First, learn to edit your own work, and work with others to make suggestions for improvement. (She has actually hired people to do this.) Second, learn what the "formula" writing is in your field, and use it to paint a good "verbal picture" of the problem you're addressing and what you're already doing to help. Don't expect that the old formulas will always work, however, and use your experience and imagination to expand formulas to be successful in new rhetorical situations. Third, don't waste your readers' time with what Weismann calls "blah blah blah" writing. Your message must compete with many other messages, so you may only have a few seconds to get the reader's attention. And finally, the public is made up of a lot of individuals. Treat them as such.

Citizens Advocate

Alan Harris is an advocate for homeless people in Atlanta, Georgia. Retired from the Social Security Administration since 1988, he began volunteering for soup kitchens in 1983. He now works primarily for the Task Force for the Homeless but describes himself as a "freelancer" who tries to work constructively with the homeless and service providers, wherever the needs are greatest. Harris's work with the homeless combines his lifelong concern about world hunger with his religious faith and commitment to public service. For years he didn't know how to express this concern "and so it lay dormant." But after attending an Atlanta-based hunger seminar he decided to "prove his resolve" by getting involved with hunger and homelessness locally.

The most gratifying aspects of Harris's work involve direct human interaction, which he believes is "the best way to find out what's going on." However, he also finds that writing can be a vital means of helping homeless people to meet their basic needs. He has written reports and conducted surveys on the problems facing shelters, and also does extensive writing on behalf of individual clients—assisting them in obtaining birth certificates or corresponding with government agencies, for example.

Harris's most extensive writing project has been to compile a directory of shelters, soup kitchens, and other programs and services designed to assist the local homeless population. He didn't particularly *want* to write this directory, he admits, but was simply responding to an urgent situation: while working at a shelter that was already filled beyond capacity, he didn't know where to send people who needed a place to stay; no centralized resource existed. Harris's work with the Social Security Administration helped him enormously with this project, providing him with the organizational skills to compile and produce the directory and the interpersonal skills to identify the problem and involve as many people as possible in its solution.

Harris knows that the documents he writes have a huge impact on the lives of homeless people, but believes that he could be an even more effective advocate if he had stronger writing skills. And although he describes his work as "a constant stream of gratifying experiences," he especially appreciates the concrete rewards, like helping someone find shelter or shoes that fit, or hearing that a client is doing well in drug treatment. While Harris acknowledges that illiteracy levels are often high among homeless people, he emphasizes that when dealing with disenfranchised groups, information needs to be shared and made accessible in ways that are convenient for the people who need it, not for the agencies that serve them.

Speech Writer

Before returning to graduate school in creative writing, Nancy Jones was Chief Speechwriter for the United States Environmental Protection Agency. In that position, she was responsible for researching and writing speeches for the administrator of the agency, and coordinating with various other offices and officials in the federal government, including the White House. When the administrator was invited to deliver a speech, Jones gathered a variety of information related to the event, which she translated into a "Speaking Engagement Profile" that she forwarded to the administrator along with his speech.

Jones got into speechwriting through prior work as a newspaper reporter as well as through volunteering for state political campaigns as a college student. This experience helped her to anticipate what questions the press might ask the administrator after his speech, and also taught her how to write under pressure and on very tight deadlines. From writing speeches, Jones learned how to write in someone else's voice and style—a skill which has helped her in her fiction—and the importance of sometimes suppressing personal opinions when representing the agency and administrator.

Although dealing with the very high level of stress and the frequent crises was one challenging part of her job, Jones admits that it was also difficult not to receive public credit for her work. The most gratifying part of her work, however, was knowing that her writing and research abilities made a difference in how issues she believed in were received by the public and opinion leaders.

```
                    SPEAKING ENGAGEMENT PROFILE
                       FOR WILLIAM K. REILLY
                          EPA ADMINISTRATOR

NAME OF GROUP:      Organization for Economic Cooperation and
                    Development (OECD), 24 Environment Ministers

LOCATION:           Paris, France

TIME AND DATE:      10 a.m., January 31, 1991

NUMBER ATTENDING:   Over 200.  Each of the 24 OECD countries is
                    sending a delegation of 5-10 people,
                    including its Environment Minister.  As you
                    know, you are heading the U.S. delegation.

THEME:              Environmental Strategy for the 1990s

OTHER SPEAKERS:     Four or five other Environment Ministers will
                    be speaking on this theme.  Speakers on the
                    first day of the conference will be
                    addressing the themes, "State of the
                    Environment" and "Integration of
                    Environmental and Economic Decision-Making."
                    You will be the first speaker on the second
                    day of the conference, to accommodate your
                    participation in President's State of the
                    Union message.  However, it is appropriate
                    and desirable for you to talk about the
                    issues raised during the first day as well.

INTRODUCING YOU:    You will put up your flag and wait to be
                    recognized.

LENGTH OF SPEECH:   Scheduled for 5 minutes, but 7 to 8 minutes
                    permissible.

ROOM SETTING:       Large, square table.  Two delegates per
                    country sit around the square.  Other
                    delegates sit behind in rows that run six
                    deep behind each side of the square.  You
                    will speak from your position at the table.

PRESS:              No press during session.  Press briefing
                    scheduled for late afternoon of January 31.
                    Speakers are invited to release longer
                    versions of their remarks to the press.  A
                    USIS wire story is being prepared based on
                    your written remarks.

OTHER:              EPA is urging OECD to initiate annual
                    environmental policy reviews for its 24
                    member countries to assure consistency and
                    coordination.
```

Figure 11.2. The categories of this Speaking Engagement Profile resemble the categories of the rhetorical situation: urgency, audience, and constraints.

Director of Web-Based Nonprofit

Paul Heavenridge is the Director of Literacyworks and the National Institute for Literacy's Literacy Information and Communication System (LINCS) based in Emeryville, California. Both are electronic clearinghouses that underwrite curriculum development related to adult and family literacy and provide curriculum materials to libraries, schools, and community organizations free of charge. Heavenridge also provides tech support for these organizations—for example, by putting curricula on-line (in multiple formats for downloading), creating websites, coordinating list-servs, and establishing audio and video streams. Although all curriculum materials are in English, Literacyworks and LINCS also publish voter guides in several languages.

Heavenridge's educational and professional background is in psychology and counseling; he has taught English overseas and worked with learning disabled adults and teen mothers. Heavenridge began to integrate technology into his curriculum after observing the potential for technology to reach non-mainstream learners by giving them confidence and delivering curriculum in ways that address diverse learning styles. He believes now more than ever that the Internet can have a positive impact on adult and family literacy development.

Heavenridge notes that finding money to support his organization can be frustrating, chiefly because it requires him to navigate the political landscape and intervene in the "pull yourself up by your bootstraps" mentality of many elected officials. Despite this, he appreciates being able to work with dedicated people who work hard despite the fact that they don't make a lot of money. Moreover, he hears inspiring stories every day about people who have achieved success through literacy acquisition.

Heavenridge recommends that anyone interested in being a professional writer get some experience doing community literacy tutoring: it teaches you how to talk to writers about writing and in the process helps you to understand writing and hone your own skills. And also learn to talk about complicated ideas and processes with people who do not know how to read or write. Finally, he encourages anyone interested in community literacy work to become proficient in multimedia platforms, because people learn in all sorts of ways.

Communications Director

Jason Mark is the Communications Director for Global Exchange, an international human rights group based in San Francisco, California. Mark's primary responsibility is to get the word out about his organization's campaigns and concerns. Toward that end, he publicizes nationwide speaking tours, edits the organization's quarterly newsletter, and edits and maintains most of the content of the Global Exchange website. He also writes (and sometimes cowrites) press releases and press advisories; public service announcements for radio, newspapers, and community calendars; and opinion pieces for placement in various media.

Before accepting his current position, Mark earned a degree in international relations and worked as a reporter, but he eventually grew frustrated by the constraints of mainstream journalism and his own self-described "armchair radicalism." Despite his journalism experience, Mark's greatest challenge as a writer is breaking through the "media noise." Scoring a mention in the mainstream media is not an end in itself, however; its real purpose is to "drive people to our website," where Mark is less restricted in his message and can therefore move beyond easily digested soundbites to writing with greater depth and complexity. Website traffic can triple after a mention in the media, and this, he says, tells him whether his message was effective.

The motto of Global Exchange—"Education for Action"—directly influences Mark's decisions as a writer. It's not enough to make a problem sound urgent, he emphasizes; you must also give the audience a next step, a concrete action that can remedy the situation and not waste their time. He finds that succinct, action-oriented, emotionally resonant writing is generally the most effective way to communicate his group's message and keep his audience's attention.

Mark acknowledges that there aren't always clear-cut successes with advocacy writing. Some days he has to be content with supportive e-mail messages from people who have visited his organization's website, many of whom describe "conversion experiences" in which their minds were changed after reading something Mark had written. These moments of human connection, he believes, can sustain the democratic values his organization seeks to promote.

Community Activists

Mark Rauscher and Billy Barwick are Co-Chairs of the Wilmington, North Carolina, chapter of the Surfrider Foundation, an international organization dedicated to beach conservation. The acronym guiding the Surfrider mission is "CARE": conservation, activism, research, and education. Members fulfill this mission by doing presentations at schools, setting up information booths at local fairs and festivals, sponsoring beach clean-ups, and lobbying for environmentally friendly legislation. Rauscher is also a graduate student in coastal geology and frequently presents his research findings at Surfrider meetings.

Because Rauscher has access to e-mail and the Internet, he is responsible for much of the writing and correspondence for the local Surfrider chapter. The national organization sponsors an e-mail listserv for local chapters to discuss issues, ask questions, or solicit ideas from other members. Rauscher monitors these discussions and forwards relevant information to local Surfriders. He also writes articles describing chapter activities for Surfrider's newsletter, *Making Waves*, maintains the local chapter's website, and writes letters and press releases. Rauscher solicits feedback and approval from other members before publishing any writing on behalf of the organization.

Since they interact with government agencies such as the Department of Natural Resources, Barwick and Rauscher have access to information that doesn't necessarily make it onto the news. They bring this information to other members and use it to formulate activist agendas. In addition to "phone-ins," where Surfrider members call politicians and encourage them to support environmentally friendly legislation, Barwick and Rauscher have also organized letter writing parties, at which they provide newspaper clippings related to coastal issues and sample letters of concern that members can consult in order to communicate effectively with local, state, and national politicians.

Barwick and Rauscher got involved in Surfider because of their mutual love of surf-ing and the coast, but both admit that activism can be draining: it's difficult to keep up with the paperwork, and efforts often fail. Barwick remains active in the organization because it allows him to channel his frustration with beach degrada-tion in positive ways. Rauscher—who jokingly describes himself as a "full-time surfer, part-time worker"—says he wants to be able not just to study the coast but do something to preserve it. "I love the coast and I'm totally saturated in it," says Rauscher. "It's all that I do." Although Rauscher and Barwick are gratified by such large-scale victories as influencing national legislation, they also cite the impor-tance of smaller successes, like when someone thanks them for making the beach a place that everyone can enjoy.

Interpreter/Translator

Adriana Weisz is a self-employed English-to-Spanish interpreter/translator in Little-ton, Colorado. She was born and raised in Argentina but has lived in the United States since 1989 and became "a proud American citizen" in 2001. Weisz has a bache-lor's degree in translation and interpretation and certification as a Federal Court In-terpreter, and is accredited by the American Translators Association; she has over 35 years of experience in this field.

As Weisz explains it, interpretation is oral and translation is written. Interpretation can be simultaneous (e.g., during conferences or hearings), consecutive (e.g., during testification of witnesses), or sight (e.g, reading aloud a document that has been pre-sented as evidence). Translation work is done for written documents and literature and should always be proofread and edited by another accredited translator. Accord-ing to Weisz, the fact that a person is fully bilingual is not sufficient for that person to be either an interpreter or a translator, "just like having two hands doesn't make you a pianist." The certification and accreditation processes are extremely difficult and require extensive experience and preparation. Unfortunately, many people don't recognize this and attempt to translate or interpret with disastrous or even dangerous consequences.

Most of Weisz's work takes place in federal courts and associated agencies; she also works for the Department of Human Services assisting with interviews at the Crisis Center, family therapy sessions, and home visits. Although Weisz does not write many original documents (outside of routine paperwork), much of her work involves the translation of such documents as letters, birth certificates, complex court documents, and brochures. Therefore she must be familiar with a wide variety of public genres and their conventions within diverse cultural settings.

Because illiteracy and lack of education are common among the Spanish-speaking people for whom she interprets, Weisz must often adjust the language level when transferring the message from English into Spanish, without altering the meaning of the source language. She notes, moreover, that many of her Spanish-speaking clients lack the concepts for certain words—particularly those in the legal context—even if they have the benefit of an interpreter; this creates a barrier to justice as well as to communication and is the cause of frequent misunderstandings. Because of these challenges, Weisz must clearly understand the message received from the Spanish speaker, which is often expressed in a very primitive form of language. In turn, she must convey to these members of the public the message received from English speakers, who may not be aware of the cultural and educational differences that affect the communication process. Successfully navigating these obstacles, she says, is "the most gratifying part of my job."

Conclusions

Clearly, there are many overlaps in these job descriptions: people who write grants might need to prepare reports or train volunteers; people who work in politics might find themselves raising money or writing press releases as well as "cleaning toilets," as one person put it. One reason for this is that jobs that serve public interests are often located in the nonprofit sector, where erratic budgets and large volunteer staffs necessitate more flexible roles and organizational structures.

The careers described here represent only a few of those available to people who have incorporated public literacy into their professional as well as their personal lives. From librarians to lobbyists, public writers play a consequential (if often invisible) role in our lives. But the important thing to remember is that any issue can be a public issue, and any career can inspire public writing. With your eyes and ears open and your notebook handy, you can write your way into public life and shape the public issues of this millennium.

Exercise

Locate a person in your community whose job involves public writing; it need not be someone who works in a position described here. Then, arrange to interview them about the kind of writing they do. The profiles for this chapter were based on the following questionnaire, which you may wish to adapt:

Name: _____

Job Title: _____

Employer: _____

1. Please describe your job. What are your primary responsibilities? What kinds of writing do you do?

2. What personal, educational, work, and/or volunteer experiences prepared you for this job?

3. What have you learned about writing from your job? What have you learned about working with the public?

4. What are the most challenging parts of your job? What are the most gratifying?